Children Apart

Children Apart

How Parents Can Help Young Children Cope with Being Away from the Family

Peter Rowlands

FOREWORD BY JOHN BOWLBY

Pantheon Books

A Division of Random House, New York

First American Edition

Copyright © 1973 by Peter Rowlands

All rights reserved under International and Pan-American Copyright Conventions. Published in the United States by Pantheon Books, a division of Random House, Inc., New York. Originally published in Great Britain as *Children Apart: Problems of Early Separation from Parents* by J. M. Dent & Sons Ltd., London.

Library of Congress Cataloging in Publication Data

Rowlands, Peter.
Children Apart.

Bibliography: p. 143-5
   1.   Parental deprivation. I.   Title.
BF723.D4R68   1974   649'.14'6   73-19218
ISBN 0-394-49212-9

Manufactured in the United States of America

Contents

Author's Acknowledgments   vi

Foreword by John Bowlby   vii

1   Children Apart: why bother about it?   1

2   Short-term Stay in Hospital I: Problems   16

3   Short-term Stay in Hospital II: the Influences that Matter   25

4   Long-term Stay in Hospital   42

5   Family Break-up I: General   59

6   Family Break-up II: Some Advice   70

7   Fostering and Adoption   79

8   Boarding-schools   96

9   Mental Handicap and Mental Disturbance   115

10   What can a Parent do about Separation?   134

References and Bibliography   143

Index   147

Author's Acknowledgments

I am indebted to a large number of people for helping me prepare this book. In the first place there are all those who consented to be interviewed, and who agreed to my seeing and talking to their children. These encounters are the mainspring of each chapter. I am particularly grateful to those who were willing, provided there was suitable disguise, for their experiences to be used as case history material.

There are also many nurses, social workers, doctors, teachers, officials in hospitals, and in central and local government, solicitors, psychologists and other experts in their own fields who have given a great deal of help. Some have clearly stated their wish, for professional reasons, to remain anonymous: but they are not forgotten.

Especially helpful were the following, who gave up a lot of their time to discuss the detail of my book, and to make important suggestions: Elizabeth Collingbridge, Dr Norman Dixon, Peggie Everard, Elizabeth Friend, Miss P. Frohlich, Roy Langmaid, Dickie Redgers, James Robertson, Marjorie Rowbottom, Beatrix Tudor-Hart. My special thanks to Ursula and John Bowlby.

October 1972.   P. R.

Foreword

Probably every parent wishes to see his, or her, child grow up to be a contented, self-reliant individual, able to make his own way in the world and able, too, to marry happily and bring up contented self-reliant children of his own. On the product to be aimed at there is usually close agreement. On how it is to be achieved, by contrast, there are still many opinions. This is unfortunate and confusing—but hardly surprising. Human beings are immensely complex—the most complex of all complex creatures here on earth—and for only a couple of generations has there been any concerted attempt to study how they develop. Small wonder therefore that so much remains unknown.

Yet from the many studies now completed certain broad conclusions can be drawn. Children thrive best when they are brought up in a stable family in which two parents are able to give them a great deal of care and attention, encouraging them, on the one hand, to develop their own life and interests and providing them, on the other, with a secure base to which they can return and in which they will always find comfort and support. Paradoxical though it may appear at first sight, self-reliance grows best in a home in which the children can rely on the unquestioning support of both their parents (or parent substitutes).

In this book Peter Rowlands describes some of the difficulties that arise when, for one reason or another, children find themselves cut off from this support; he also outlines measures that parents can take to forestall difficulties and mitigate them should they develop. In the personal stories he tells of how particular children fared, first when they were parted from their parents and, later, when they had returned home, many simple yet basic principles are illustrated.

Since losing a parent's support, either temporarily or permanently, is extremely distressing for a child, it is to be expected that every child will be alarmed by anything he construes as a threat that he may be abandoned. Most parents recognize this and are determined to say and do nothing that might give that impression. Unfortunately, however, there is a minority who are less careful, and still all too many who use threats to abandon a child or to withdraw love as disciplinary measures. Plainly, to expose a child to such threats, wittingly or unwittingly, can do nothing but harm. Should such a child subsequently be separated from his parents for any reason the harm done will be multiplied many times over. For in such circumstances it is inevitable that he will construe the separation as the punishment that was threatened; and so, in addition to the distress, he will experience it as something for which he himself is to blame.

There is now good reason to believe that the guilt that certain children experience in connection with a separation, and that is described so clearly in this book, is to be attributed either to the deliberate threats or else to the unguarded remarks that their parents have made during preceding months and years. Perhaps the best precaution that parents can take to mitigate the ill-effects attendant on an unavoidable separation, therefore, is to make sure that in no circumstances has a child ever been exposed to threats, explicit or veiled, of being abandoned by them.

In a difficult area such as this there are bound to be points about which there are differences of opinion. One such is on the theme of what Peter Rowlands calls 'mini-separations'. In the first chapter it reads as though he believes it to be necessary for a child as young as a year old to be exposed to mini-separations and that, if he were not, he would never learn to tolerate being away from his parents. I am sure any such view is mistaken. Naturally, it is a good insurance policy for a child to have one or two other familiar persons to whom he could turn should his parents be unavailable. But becoming familiar with other people, who would be able if necessary to act as reserve caretakers, is best done in mother's presence, not in her absence. Given unfailing security during his early years a child needs no pressing to extend his range of acquaintances and experiences: indeed he becomes impatient for them. Trying to hustle him forward is all too apt to have the reverse effect.

Naturally, all children are different and so are all parents. The best of books can do no more than give parents a better to understanding of how children are made and in what sorts of environment they thrive. Just how parents apply this knowledge they must themselves decide. I believe this book will help many to understand better why, whenever possible, separations are to be avoided and, when that is not possible, how best the disturbances that follow can be dealt with.

1973.   JOHN BOWLBY.

One
Children Apart:
why bother about it?

In many ways it seems almost banal to be writing a book about how important family life and maternal affection are for children. Of course children should be close to their mothers, and of course not having a mother can influence a child's later life. Isn't this what most people have known all along?

There are a number of good reasons for tackling the subject, particularly now.

For one thing the number of children who are at risk of losing a sense of what it is to have a parent, and whose family life is under threat, is growing markedly. Medical expertise has developed faster than our ability to deal with some of the consequences. These include both the many children who manage to survive abnormality at birth, and the many more who are coaxed back to life after accidents and serious illnesses. Lots of these children require special medical and psychiatric care, which need to be professionally supplied: but must they forgo home life for existence in an institution?

Then again the number of young children who are subject to some kind of compromise arrangement, or judicial decision in divorce proceedings, has just about trebled in the United Kingdom over the past ten years. In fact there are probably fewer of these than there are children allotted in one direction or other after an unrecorded separation of husband and wife. Many children in these two circumstances may remain with at least one parent—or they may not. Whichever the result is, they increase the number who can be said to be at risk of premature separation.

But separation need not be very long for it to be dangerous, and worth considering carefully. For a very young child, a short visit to a hospital can be extremely disturbing. Similarly, entry into a boarding-school, for the child who is emotionally unprepared for it, can make a profound impression within a relatively short space of time.

All these considerations seemed to make it worth approaching separation of child from parent as a subject in its own right, given that it takes many complex forms. This book is trying to help parents, by examining the commonest of these forms in some detail and putting them into a theoretical context.

Apart from offering individuals some advice, it seemed worth while underlining some basic social problems as well.

For instance, the present decade may prove to be a particularly significant one in the care provided for children in hospitals. The proportion of hospitals where allowance is made for unrestricted visiting by mothers, or for them to come in with their young children to stay, is still a minority. But the tide is such that the recognition of the importance of family contact may become less of a pious official hope and more of a general reality.

At the same time, there are clear-cut official pronouncements favouring community care for children who have to receive medical care for long periods, as opposed to indefinite committal to institutions. If this is felt to warrant at least some official expenditure and pressure, these views may bear fruit. But meanwhile the *slowness* of change is taking its toll, in terms of dehumanization.

It is perhaps not too cruel to claim that a modern society gets the kind of hospitals it deserves. Certainly, if more people expressed stronger anxieties about the physical and organizational sides of the hospital service as they affect children, it would be a greater incentive to the government of the day to put more investment into improving them. It would also influence the more intransigent, traditionalist units that have done comparatively little to conform to official recommendations on dealing with children.

Unfortunately hospitals and homes make an impact on the

public at large only when there is a scandal of sufficient pro-portions to make the headlines. At other times what goes on inside them is a series of what are regarded as purely personal encounters. This can partly be put down to the public's basic respect for an official system which they *want* and *expect* to be above reproach or criticism. It limits progress, because it is only by sufficient pressure from society that a large official system gets adapted. Without protest, inertia prevails.

A great deal depends on developing a broader understanding of what is important in a child's world; and how personality, and character traits like confidence, generosity, etc., are formed. This kind of area is sometimes carefully ignored by parents: either they prefer not to contemplate just how closely they may be accountable for much of their children's nature, or they feel that it is material for psychologists, or 'head-shrinkers', and best left to them. Against this, perhaps the most optimistic sign of the times is that more and more people are insisting on finding these things out for themselves. They observe, discuss, argue, and judge—rather than leaving it all to experts.

Premature Separation

When somebody copes with a new situation easily, it is usually because he already knows more or less what it is going to be like, or, he has encounted other situations that he can compare it with; or, he is a strong enough character to accept that new situations can occur, and that it does not help to get bothered by them. All three reasons are likely, in some combination or other, when somebody takes all kinds of events in his stride.

The basic point to be made about young children—say, from birth to five years, although the upper limit may vary a lot—is that when they are suddenly separated from their parents, none of the above reasons for success in dealing with the problem is likely to apply. It is hardly surprising, therefore, that children should often react in a dramatic way to premature separation. Nor is it really remarkable that these children should be more disturbed by separation from their mother than from their father.

In most cases she is their habitual main line of defence against the unexpected.

Because separation of a young child from his mother is sometimes convenient, sometimes necessary, and sometimes forced, this is not a point that everyone enjoys considering. But it is important to examine it, in order to work out for a given situation what is the most desirable (in some cases, the least undesirable) way of arranging the separation for the welfare of the child. There may be several courses of action open, for instance: to take time off work so that a sick child can be looked after at home, instead of in hospital; delaying an operation, where this is medically reasonable, until a child is older; waiting until he is older before putting him into a boarding-school; choosing between home and residential care for a chronically sick child; choosing appropriate fostering arrangements after a family split. In these cases, knowing about the effects of premature separation allows for better based judgment. Where there is little or no choice, it helps one realize what pointers to look for in assessing the child's circumstances and his development, and to plan what kinds of change or compensation should be pressed for.

Many have felt that however uncomfortable a week or a month might be for a child who suddenly finds himself separated, the effects of a brief separation are likely to be only temporary. Some go further and even suggest that this kind of experience can be of positive value, because it encourages self-reliance and discourages over-dependence on other people. They point to instances of famous people who had atrocious handling in their childhood but achieved wonderful things nonetheless.

Three things are worth bearing in mind when this kind of argument is being put forward, whether it is voiced by parents who are anxious to get their children into boarding-school at the earliest opportunity or by disinterested observers. The first is that famous people are not always happy people. Secondly, for every shining example of a genius who overcame some kind of abandonment early on, to flourish and impress the world, there are many others (names unknown, for obvious reasons) who have had a long and painful struggle to adjust to the world. Compensation for lack of maternal affection may well have been the goal of some who have built industrial empires out of nothing. But this has eluded the grasp of most. The high proportion of delinquents who come from broken homes and had a shuttle-service upbringing, speaks for itself. The third point is worth making, too. If one is to learn 'self-reliance', there must be a strong enough 'self' on which to rely. How this is acquired is worth considering.

When a child develops normally he makes reference points which are important to him in learning to understand and cope with what the world has to offer. Chief among these are his parents, who are constants in front of a changing scene; who react to him in ways that he gets to know and to value; who reassure and explain; who declare what is right and wrong, true and false; and who serve as convenient and safe testing grounds for new ideas or behaviour that the child feels like trying out. Having such a reference point is very important early in life, for developing (among other things) a sense of what one's own self is like, and capable of doing. Famous people who were orphaned, or abandoned by their parents, often had another relative or a foster parent who took on this individual role.

A 'reference point' is a cold, inanimate concept. Parents who are helping a child to develop have to be warm and active. They will take the lead in fashioning a close relationship, in which two people can be relaxed with each other, can say what they feel, can touch and kiss each other when they want to, can explore ideas without fear of an unfriendly reception. Having such a model of partnership, or loving, helps a child to understand and appreciate what human relationships ought, at best, to mean. This realization is used when the child builds up friendships outside the home, and when he avoids behaviour that he has learnt to be dangerous to continuing friendship.

During the years that this first, very important, relationship with an adult is being worked out anything that threatens it is naturally frightening for a child. Normally, a complete separation between a young child and his mother will happen only in circumstances where there are strong reassuring influences. These can include having father or grandmother at home while mother may be away at hospital. Or, if a child is left by parents who want to go away for a long week-end just by themselves, it can mean having an older brother or sister, in the same situation, or being looked after by neighbours whose home is very familiar ground. These are quite different cases from those where: (a) a child is taken to a strange place away from home, for several days or more; or, (b) a child is separated in such a way that the original mother-child relationship has to change.

An example of the first of these two situations would be a visit to a hospital for a week. This can be a very long time indeed in the mind of a child under five, and often for older children. An example of the second would be any arrangement that suspends direct contact indefinitely, such as fostering, or putting the child into hospital for a long time. Putting him into a boarding-school may, if he is very young, be tantamount to the same thing.

Of course separation is inevitable at some point in a person's development. But a lucky child does not reach a difficult separation situation until he is mature enough to deal with it. Maturity needs time. It also needs a variety of experience, and a reasonably successful history of coping with this experience. What usually happens is that a child becomes accustomed, over time, to a series of mini-separations. By itself, a mini-separation (any brief break in contact between mother and child) can only be discouraging. But if the arrangements for it are based on a positive extension of the child's experience of other people, and if it provides an opportunity for the child to build confidently on that extension, it can contribute towards his confidence.

At the age of one a baby may find one day that instead of his mother taking him in the pram to go shopping, he is taken to a neighbour's house. Here an older child pushes a furry toy into his hands, and a woman he just about recognizes gives him his lunch, out of a familiar bowl. Whether or not he is in a state of apprehension by the time his mother returns from a shopping expedition in the metropolis may depend very much on the confidence in handling him shown by the neighbours, and the variety of distractions that they contrive to offer him. He may cry part of the time, and he may sleep. But not very much later, his mother returns, picks him up and hugs him.

When the process is next repeated, it is likely to become an accepted variation on the normal course of life, as far as the child is concerned. In fact, all may not be completely forgiven, as many mothers have discoverd. The day following any such expedition, the child may be more stubborn and more bad-tempered than usual. Some put this down to 'paying me back, for going off and not taking him along too'. But jealousy of this kind is probably too complex a thought process for a toddler. More likely, he is demonstrating that he was worrying, that he did not like her apparent change in attitude towards being near him, and that therefore his sense of what constitutes correct behaviour, and feeling between himself and his mother, is out of gear. This would make it very similar, albeit on a small scale, to the disturbed behaviour of young children who have returned home after an alarming spell in hospital. A mini-separation has a mini-reaction.

Later the one-year-old may get left for slightly longer periods. Some of these, such as the first week-end his parents contrive to turn into a brief holiday for themselves, may be difficult for the child to accept. But in most cases, as the mini-separations pass by without anything very unpleasant happening, the increasing length of the separation periods is tolerated.

Psychologists sometimes call this learning by successive approximation. It is what we mean when we say that a young person has reached sufficient maturity, through time and experience, to be left away from his parents for a long holiday, for a school term, or whatever. This stage cannot be reached by his parents' decision, as much as by the child's gradual progress towards it. If that progress is rushed the results may be harmful.

Naturally there are other factors that complicate the picture. Not least among these is the strength of feeling that the mother has towards the child; the influence of brothers or sisters, who may encourage confidence or panic; and the fact that different children come to understand explanations of what is going on at a different pace.

But there are good reasons for supposing that if a young child undergoes a very disturbing separation before he is mature enough to take it in his stride, it can have a severe effect on him. This has a lot to say for the basic importance to a child of a solid link with his mother. But it also suggests, by implication, that when a series of mini-separations is successful, it has considerable importance in making a child feel confident when the unexpected happens.

Here are two brief examples of what premature separation can do to people. In neither of them can it be proved beyond all doubt that everything would have been fine had it not been for the separation. Life is not like that. But the situations are paralleled by a large number of similar case histories. The first relates to a short but harrowing experience. The second involves a long, embittering separation period. Together they make the point that length of time in itself is much less important to the outcome than the circumstances.

Ian

When he was nearly two years old, Ian was taken to a well-known London hospital. He had a slight hernia, which needed immediate attention. In view of his age, in case there were complications, it was felt that he ought to stay in hospital for ten days.

This was roughly twenty years ago. At that time it was not considered unusual for a hospital to bid his mother goodbye as soon as a toddler was placed physically into a nurse's arms. He screamed, but she was asked to leave at once, because 'it's for the best, you know, and it's not visiting time'. Nor was it unusual for her to be issued with a card indicating four two-hour periods during the week in which it was permitted to visit. It was quite obvious to Ian's mother whenever she visited that her son was extremely unhappy, and that attempts to see him more often were vain against a stone wall of resistance.

On return home Ian was regressive—he seemed to have lost the words he knew, and he would no longer signal when he wanted the lavatory. At night, every night, he woke with a shriek, demanding to know if his mother was there.

He grew up outwardly a normal boy. But his parents quickly realized he was very unlike his elder brother and sister. The gap between them seemed even greater after a second visit to hospital, when he was four, forced on his reluctant parents by a recurrence of hernia trouble. This was more brief, but the separation was again agonizing for Ian.

Children often have peculiar compulsions—not wanting to step on lines in the pavement is an obvious one. But these are normally short-lived. Ian would, for a time, refuse to come down in the morning before he had run his palms across the whole surface of a particular wall in his bedroom. He had to put his clothes on in a particular order every day. Changes in clothing, such as the introduction of a cardigan, at five, reduced him to panic. He was very difficult to distract from his rituals. He made it clear that he feared some kind of calamity if he did not follow them through. Removing him forcibly from the scene and telling him not to be so silly was tried. But the result was a pathetic, nervous creature, who shivered and whined, and could not apply himself to anything—sweets included.

By the age of nine he was regarded as a peculiar and unhappy boy at school. The religious instruction there made a deep impression on him. He began to need to stop what he was doing and mouth prayers under his breath before going on. Railway stations, department stores—any large building with lots of people—made him very anxious: he would stop and say a prayer in the street before allowing himself to be led in.

Two psychiatrists were asked to advise on how to help Ian. They arrived independently at a very similar conclusion. Ian, they decided, had never properly recovered from the shock of hospital and losing contact with his mother. He was not *aware* of why he was afraid of big buildings, or why he felt the need to protect himself by organizing his life neatly, and praying. These feelings simply dominated him. One of the psychiatrists managed to reassure him about his fear of God who, white-coated and more powerful than his parents, had strong associations with those who had seized him and terrified him long before.

With self-awareness, and the ability to talk about the past with his parents, Ian gained in confidence. From about twelve on-wards, he became progressively more like his brother. He has just graduated from university.

The problems that children have with hospitalization are examined in the next three chapters. Ian is by no means alone in the way he seems to have been affected, although not all young children who are badly disturbed by a visit to hospital show long-term effects that are quite so obvious, or so unfortunate.

The point of introducing Karen's case history at this stage is to show how a long-term separation of a young child from her parents—when it is she alone, and not her sister, who is hived off—can have lasting, tragic effects. In her case it is worth noting that the character Karen developed in reaction to the separation was scarcely affected by any of the factors that might normally be considered likely to compensate. Staying with grandmother, going to a boarding-school with an easy atmosphere, educa-tional success, reunion with the family, the mother's determina-tion to have a close, happy family again after the separation—all these must have contributed something, but not enough.

Karen

In the early years of World War II, Karen's mother took her younger daughter, Philippa, to the Far East. Karen, who was three, was left behind, to stay with her grandmother in Scotland. Taking both children would have been difficult, and expensive. The elder daughter was felt to be the logical one to leave behind. Karen's father was with the British Army, and since Japan had not yet entered the war joining him seemed a safe enough thing to do. It was explained to Karen (or, rather, she was *told* this) that once the war was over, which no one doubted would be soon, they would all meet up again in Scotland.

Those who knew Karen at this time describe her as being utterly disconsolate for a number of days. Then she allowed herself to become interested in what was going on at the farm which was at the end of the lane from her grandmother's home. Elaborate arrangements were made to get her to meet other children. She would play with them, although she was not demonstratively friendly. She smiled more, and laughed. A kind of 'settling down' seemed to be taking place.

Letters from abroad were hard to come by during the war. When any did arrive, Karen's grandmother tried to make it a special event. Karen would pay attention obediently when the letters were read out, then turn to her toys or to the dog.

Later it was obvious that Karen wanted no information about her mother or sister. She only had to catch sight of a letter that had an 'Opened by Censor' mark down one side, to be off along the lane to the farm. Despite being an early reader, she never showed any desire to read these letters herself.

The depth of her feelings may be judged from a strange confrontation she had with her sister shortly after the end of the war. Karen was then nine, and Philippa nearly seven.

Philippa had to make entirely new friends on her return to Scotland. She found herself cold-shouldered at first, but being extrovert, and having a lot to talk about, she broke down her sister's friends' reserve. The big problem was that Karen ignored her almost completely. Persistently, Philippa followed Karen about, imitating her, trying to join in, trying to ask questions that she would answer. Eventually Philippa found herself seized by the throat, and shaken. Karen stared at her but did not in fact hurt Philippa, who had the impression later that her sister disliked touching her. 'I will never be friends with you,' Karen declared. 'And I will always hate you. Always.'

It sounds melodramatic—almost comic. Children often make such pronouncements, only to forget them a day or so afterwards. But the rift between Karen and Philippa was permanent. Years later, when Philippa joined her sister at boarding-school, Karen (then fourteen) made her position clear again.

Avoiding her mother was less easy than avoiding her sister. Karen's mother realized very quickly after her return that she had a struggle ahead. It was not made easier by the fact that her husband had died, on service. But she tried hard. She went for a short holiday alone, just with Karen. When Karen fell ill with chicken-pox, she did her best to take on the whole job of nursing her, and distracting her from scratching. When Karen was being particularly distant she tried making a bridge to her by tickling her and kissing her, and laughing as she urged her daughter to 'snap out of it'. Sometimes it seemed to work—but never completely, or lastingly. Karen learned to take refuge from her mother's attentions in books and homework. She was delighted when told she could at last, after many requests, go to boarding-school.

Karen's mother felt a certain respect for her daughter's independence of will and spirit. She was pleased that she was obviously clever at school. Karen, she felt, must be a strong character. Here she was mistaken.

The following years need to be telescoped. Karen made few friends. Her intense way of looking at people and her suspicious nature were rather forbidding. But she studied well, and went to university—the first of her family to do so. There she met a man who fell in love with her. She accepted his proposal of marriage, on condition that they did it quickly and quietly, at a registry office in Oxford. She could not prevent her mother coming up to attend the degree ceremony, but she made amends two weeks later by sending a postcard from London with the casual information that she was now married, and on honeymoon.

Karen had two children in quick succession. She quarrelled frequently with her husband: at first it was mainly about money and about 'being tied to the children', but later she took to accusing him of adultery, or perversion, of being a crook. . . .

Her husband, who claimed later that he had never been able 'to get through' to his wife, despite five years of marriage, and two children, was gradually attracted elsewhere. He feels that she has always concealed part of herself from view.

For the past ten years Karen has alternated between periods of wanting to get control again of her children, and mental disturbance of a kind which means that she has, for a while, to abandon contact with them, and attend courses of treatment. For a few months she will be determined to get things right this time, to care for her children properly, to be a success at living independently, to make friends and to be happy. For a while it works.

But it does not take much (it is not clear, precisely, what) to change her into her other role. This is when she ignores the children, and suffers great agitation. She fears she has to travel, to be on the run, to move anywhere. This is usually followed by a longer period of deep depression. Various drugs have helped her, and she has come to rely on them rather than on human support. A big problem for her ex-husband is working out how they should divide the decision-making for their children.

The children, now at boarding-school, seem remarkably well adjusted, and objective about their parents. They like and have sympathy for their mother and for their father, because they have been ill, or had problems. . . . It is tempting to suggest that separation caused by illness and problems that the children can partly understand is more easily forgiven than if it seems to be a result of the parents' whim or preference.

*   *   *

Neither Ian nor Karen properly understood what was being done, and why, when they were taken into unfamiliar surroundings and dumped. This may seem an unfair description, but if the children saw anything they probably saw it that way. One can only guess at the further interpretation that the children put on the separation event. Ian may have felt that his mother lost control of him, possibly through negligence, possibly through lack of power. Karen may have believed that her sister was supplanting her entirely in her parents' eyes. This is pure speculation—but it illustrates the kind of train of thought which, however hazy, may colour the child's view.

Sometimes a child gets the impression that the separation that is forced on him is a kind of punishment. This is more common when the child is old enough to have a general awareness that such a thing as punishment actually happens, but not old enough to understand an explanation that he is given. If he feels particularly guilty about something, obviously the chances of a punishment interpretation are enhanced. This is not quite the same as making a deduction that one is being rejected, which also sometimes happens to a child who suddenly feels left alone. But the two interpretations can, logically, merge.

This is by no means as far-fetched as it may appear at first. Children whose parents fall ill are often perplexed about them. 'But why does Mummy have to go away?' is often asked several times over, even when the words of explanation from Daddy seem to have been sinking in. Children may then reveal a fear that something they have done may be partly responsible, particularly, for instance, if they have been warned not to be so noisy near Mummy's bedroom. This kind of guilty feeling is extremely difficult for a child to live with, and is well worth taking trouble to discover, and then work on until it is rooted out.

Another point to consider at this stage is the availability of a mother substitute. Karen's grandmother, for various reasons, failed to fulfil this role entirely satisfactorily. In Ian's case, the circumstances were not propitious for anyone to be a very satisfactory substitute. Two separate issues are involved: sometimes the circumstances are against a mother substitute, and sometimes the individual trying to act as one cannot succeed. There are infinite combinations. But it is almost always better for somebody, however inadequate, to attempt and continue person-to-person communication with a child who is undergoing premature separation than to give it up as a bad job.

Both of the studies given so far are depressing. Ian, admittedly, has made progress. But considerable harm has been done to him, and this cannot be undone. Karen's life history seems particularly sad, in that other people have been unhappily involved in it. But the two studies present a kind of challenge. If, by understanding more about young children and their needs, this kind of problem can be lessened or avoided, then the challenge is really worth while accepting.

The aim of this book is not to depress but to help. To do this, however, means pointing out some of the dangers of premature separation. It is only against this background that any recommendations on what to do and what to avoid become at all meaningful.

The points of view put forward here are well noted in academic and clinical observations. Many different sources contribute. Freud's work on the important effects early experiences have in later life; experimental studies of the effects of deprivation of maternal care on young animals—for example, by Harlow; the work of the Tavistock Institute, over the past three decades, on the whole mother-child relationship; and the work of ethologists on instincts in mother-and-child behaviour—all can be appealed to as authoritative. But what happens to people, in what circumstances, is the mainspring.

Two
Short-term Stay in Hospital
I: Problems

There are a great number of situations in which it is open to the parents to decide whether they will be separated from their young child or not. Sometimes this applies to hospitalization, but more often the need for a child to go into hospital is sudden and unpredictable. This is typically the case with short-term stay in hospital, which may be defined as a visit lasting from one day to about a month.

If there is an urgent reason why a young child must have immediate treatment in hospital which may last a few days, or more, there is little more to do than to propel him in the direction of the nearest available hospital that will do the job. Nothing that is written in this or the next chapter should be taken as contradicting this basic point that a child's important health needs must be given first priority.

But a child has mental health needs as well. This means that it is always worth knowing in advance what are the attitudes and practice at local hospitals towards safeguarding children's welfare in its broader aspects. It also means being prepared to take steps to help a young child *as a parent*. Both these points are expanded later. The net results should be that instead of standing dumbly by, when the doctor recommends that a two-year-old should be taken at once to Hospital X for observation, the parent should be able to respond like this:

'Does it matter, Doctor, if he goes into Hospital Y instead of X?'

'Well, no. I suppose not. Why?'

'They've got arrangements for mothers to go in overnight there. And they believe in unrestricted visiting.'

Knowing about local practice can help in an emergency, because you know automatically what you are up against. It is also well worth while working out, *before* an emergency happens, how to arrange for the rest of the family to be looked after if mother has to accompany the youngest into hospital. Which of the relatives or the neighbours would co-operate? Would father be able to cope? Would he get the older children off to school on time? What would be the best way to make sure the other children didn't feel excluded or disregarded? With a reasonable amount of luck this contingency plan need never be put into effect. But it's worth making just in case—for peace of mind, and also to be able to advise other parents who are less lucky.

There is also a whole range of predicaments where action is not needed immediately. For example, a four-year-old could have his tonsils out in a few months' time. It's not absolutely essential. It could wait. Meanwhile, you can wait for him to get older, to understand things better, and you can cast about for the best place in which he can have his operation, according to criteria which will be discussed later.

Preparations in advance will always repay. Some of the main reasons will become clear in the case histories of two children who had very different experiences in hospital—Robin and Nicholas.

They may have been different from each other before they were admitted to their hospitals, but they are absolutely representative of large numbers of children who pass through the swing doors of traditionalist, or progressive, wards respectively.

Robin and Nicholas in hospital

When Robin was just four years old, his family's doctor strongly recommended that he should have an operation for adenoids— the sooner the better. His mother was told that this would mean his going into hospital for about ten days. This worried her, and she queried whether it would not be better to wait until Robin was a bit older. No, was the reply. His adenoid condition might be indirectly affecting his hearing; it might stop him from becoming fully fit; and it might get more difficult to treat surgically.

He was accepted into M hospital a couple of months later. When he arrived, he was pleased that something was going to be done 'to help his nose feel all better again', but he was apprehensive, at the same time.

Suddenly he found himself being kissed by his mother, and being told, 'Goodbye, Robin; Mummy will be back very soon.' For a while he did not fully comprehend the meaning of this. He registered surprise at being undressed and given a bath. His eyes were very big, and he peered round with alarm. The nurse who was seeing to him, however, was brisk, and commanded immediate respect. He co-operated with her.

But when he was brought back, in pyjamas, to the children's ward, and told, 'There's your bed, then, Robin—hop in!', he felt panic. His mother was simply not there.

The nurse who watched and recorded these events mentioned that Robin did not even reach the bed under his own steam. He seemed to crumple to the floor, shaking with loud sobs of despair. An older boy nearby sneered a derisive, 'Oh no!' The nurse who had bathed him picked him up bodily and settled him firmly in bed. 'Don't be silly, Robin,' she said. 'You'll have some lovely lunch in a few minutes. And your mummy will be back to see you very, very soon.'

In fact, his mother was not allowed in to see him the next day, which was the day of the operation. She was told by telephone that Robin was quite all right. 'He was fretful at first. Most of them are, of course. But he settled down very quickly, and the operation was fine.'

When his mother again reached the ward she noticed that he was sitting up in bed, his head supported by two pillows, solemnly regarding a toy lorry, and detaching its wheels. She felt relieved. 'Well, he looks all right, anyway,' she said to herself.

But when Robin saw her he began to cry loudly. A nurse came up to hold him still, gesturing to his mother to keep away. 'You've disturbed him, I'm afraid,' she commented curtly.

A few days passed before Robin accepted his mother's visits tranquilly. He was difficult when she left to go, but in time even this happened without a protest on his part.

By now he felt braver with the other 'up' children. He was deep in conversation with another boy about how best to fit together the pieces of a wooden fortress when his mother arrived to take him home.

'Hello, Robin!' She hugged him. 'Come on, you're coming home.'

'Oh.' He looked rather disappointed. 'But I've got this fortress.'

His mother remarked to his father that evening that it was wonderful how cheerful and relaxed their son was. 'Really, we shouldn't have worried so much.'

But it was not yet over.

That evening when told it was bedtime he threw a tantrum. It was on a scale they had not experienced since he was a two-year-old. Now, of course, he was stronger and louder.

This was the first of many tantrums. He also distinguished himself by tearing as much wallpaper as he could off his bedroom wall; refusing to eat anything that was not fish fingers or ice-cream; pulling the spines off his mother's cookery books; breaking the heads, arms and legs off all the toy soldiers he had been given for Christmas; and throwing the kitten over the fire-guard, so that it singed its fur against the base of the electric fire. Not all at once, of course: over several weeks.

'Something changed between my son and me,' his mother claimed in an interview. 'He was a very cuddly baby, and he was all for hugs and kisses as a toddler too. But when he came back from hospital he seemed quite different. He wanted me sometimes all right. But most of the time he seemed to want to pay me back.'

His father demanded action. He insisted that his wife go down and visit the hospital and find out what had been going on there.

She did so, and had one very unsatisfactory meeting with the ward sister, who implied that she must either be an incompetent mother, or getting worked up over nothing. Fortunately, however, the ward sister passed her on quickly to the student nurse who had been able to observe Robin during his first days. This nurse discussed all she had noticed, sympathetically. A number of points came to light. No solution appeared, but it helped Robin's mother to talk about the problem.

It took time for the family to regain the happy spirit it once had. Robin's father took a big part in this. He spent more time with his son at week-ends, and got him interested in the local football team, and in flying kites.

A year later, things were going so well that the hospital and its aftermath were practically forgotten. Robin's mother might even have stopped believing that the episode had had any long-term effect had it not been for one curious event.

Robin's grandmother fell and broke her thigh. She too was taken to M hospital. One afternoon, Robin was told they would go and visit Gran, who had hurt her leg. When they got on a different bus from the one that usually took them to Gran's house he was slightly surprised, but said nothing. As soon as they were stepping off the bus, he saw the building that he remembered all too well. 'We're going to the hospital' had meant nothing to him. But the façade, and the nurses' uniforms by the front gate, meant a great deal. He screamed, dropped the box of chocolates he was carrying, and struggled to get into the bus.

At about the same time that Robin had his hospital experience, Nicholas half-swallowed a pin, which lodged in the lower part of his throat. Also four years old, he was in some discomfort and alarm when his mother took him to the Casualty Ward at H hospital. X-rays were taken, studied, and carefully examined by an ear, nose and throat specialist, while they waited.

'I'm afraid Nicholas ought to stay in overnight. He needs an operation, and the earliest we can do that is tomorrow morning.'

Nicholas's mother made it clear that she was very worried about leaving her son. The sister in charge of the children's ward was very helpful. She suggested that Nicholas's mother should stay with him until a pain-killing injection took effect; that she should telephone her neighbours, to ask them to watch out for

Nicholas's elder sister when she got home from school; that she should telephone her husband at work, and ask him to collect a case containing pyjamas, toothbrush, and so forth. Everything went more or less according to plan. Nicholas's mother was encouraged to stay on and take her evening meal by her son's bedside.

'The important thing is for him not to get too upset when he wakes up,' the sister stressed.

'If he wakes up in the middle of the night——' Nicholas's mother did not finish her sentence. Her tone made it quite clear what she was worrying about, and how much she was worrying. Nicholas might wake up, and find himself in a strange place, without his mother: he would not understand why, how, for how long. . . .

The children's ward was small, even cramped, but at one end was a set of camp-beds, folded up and clamped to the wall. 'It won't be very comfortable, I'm afraid,' said the sister, 'but you're welcome to use a camp-bed. There's just room for one between the beds. Mrs Blake, over there, has been over-nighting on one.'

Next morning Nicholas held his mother's hand during the 'pre-med' arrangements, and she was allowed to help push his trolley right up to the doors of the operating theatre. When he regained consciousness after his operation the first thing he heard in the Recovery Room was his mother's voice, and he soon felt her hand around his.

His mother had to go home that day, but Nicholas seemed confident about his surroundings. He accepted that his mother would not be away for long. The sister made it clear, in his hearing, that his mother could come and go just as she pleased.

There was a complicating infection after Nicholas's operation, which needed further medical care. It was some time before he could eat normally, and his recovery was slower than expected. But the nurse who was 'specialed' to him reported that he kept very cheerful.

When Nicholas was brought home, he settled down comfortably. There was no problem when he was told later that he needed to go back to H hospital, to have his throat checked again. Everything about his behaviour suggested that, although he had

had a difficult and somewhat painful time, this was all chalked up to experience in his mind.

* * *

Robin's and Nicholas's histories are typical of what can happen, given particular circumstances.

There are many factors that may have been incidental. For instance, Nicholas's temperament, perception and maturity may have been better suited to hospitalization than Robin's. But there is enough evidence from other sources to suggest that the crucial factor is likely to have been whether mother and child were separated or not—at critical stages of his visit. This will be analysed in Chapter 3.

At this point, it is worth underlining that Robin's case may not be over yet. It is now nearly four years since he was in hospital for adenoids. His mother feels that, although they are much closer now than they were immediately after his return home, Robin has never become quite the same. Two years ago she had her second child, Patrick, of whom Robin has been consistently jealous and suspicious. Robin is called a 'loner' by his teacher at primary school. He resents group activities, and tends to be destructive.

On the credit side, he works well at school by himself, and despite having only moderate concentration is taking more trouble about the models he makes, and the projects he begins. His liking for his father is strong; he looks forward to seeing him, and they get on well.

Everything is being done to avoid it but Robin may be carrying some of his separation problems with him through life. This is by no means uncommon. In one sense, Robin is lucky, because other children have been very seriously affected indeed by separation. Research evidence points to the probability that if he had been two years younger when he went to hospital, the after-effects would have been significantly worse.

Age, and the other factors that seem to be particularly important in affecting the issue, are discussed in the next chapter. Some of them suggest practical measures in themselves, because by knowing about them parents can take appropriate action. Others are less easy to act on, such as the principle that anxiety is communicated from parent to child. If a mother is being very anxious about the visit to hospital and makes this obvious to her child, he would be unnatural if he did not start worrying himself. This could mean that he is more likely to put sinister interpretations on what is said and done to him there. But you cannot simply tell a mother to be less nervous, if she is nervous by nature, particularly if she is very concerned about her child's illness. The only advice that *does* make sense, in this context, is to stop alarming the child by displaying her own alarm.

There are not many books written about the role that mothers or parents should play in hospital. (Two good ones are mentioned at the end of this book.) It may seem strange that, if premature separation in the hospital situation is important, it has not been accorded as much attention as, say, measles, or physiotherapy. The reasons are complex.

In under-developed countries, while hospitals may not be very clean or attractive, it is very often automatic for a parent to accompany a child—or any sick relative for that matter—into hospital and look after him. As medical standards rise, elimination of anything that threatens the maintenance of antiseptic conditions becomes the rule. So does a sense of strict professionalism which tends to demand exclusive rights and responsibilities in caring for, as well as treating, a patient. Visitors become suspect because they are foreign to the system. It is a short step from this to the view that the medical profession must know best, and must therefore defend the work of the hospital against interference from any source. Ignorant interference is, by definition, dangerous.

A number of eminent medical experts have queried, from time to time, whether hospitals had not gone too far in developing a rigid barrier between 'them' and 'us', particularly in children's wards. Some of them applied their beliefs in a practical way, adapting the regulations of children's wards over which they had control so as to strike a compromise between medical demands and the child's demands for a close link with his home.

But they have met with suspicion and disagreement. The trend is in their favour, but it is a long process.

Anything so long-term, variable and shapeless as maternal care is very difficult to measure, either in itself or in its effects. The same applies to deprivation, or premature separation. Modern man has learned to believe in what can be measured. Psychology fascinates him, but is suspected by him for this reason. What precise value can be put on influences that form part of the background to life?

Unfortunately, mental health problems are real, despite being so difficult to measure. They are with us, and require psychology to analyse them, and the influences that bear on them. The analysis may need to be tentative, but we owe it to ourselves to try to make it.

Three
Short-term Stay in Hospital
II: The Influences that Matter

Robin and Nicholas had different experiences, for a number of reasons. Before going into these reasons in detail, here are some general points that can influence the situation.

Both these children were mentally normal. If either of them had not been he might have come off very badly. What is puzzling to an ordinary child may be even more alarming to one who has difficulty in understanding what is happening at home. Anyone who has taken such a child to undergo medical tests at a hospital may well recognize this. As often as not the same medical staff who took him over so confidently at the beginning return to his mother asking if she will come and help. She does—and she usually can help, provided it is not left too late. This parallels what often happens with young normal children who have to stay by themselves in hospital for a few days. They can have more explained to them, but then the bizarre fact of mother's disappearance—if she leaves them—breaks down their defences, and their capacity to be reassured. Their mother may not return, except for brief, inexplicably short periods. They have to adjust painfully to a new concept of the world, and to a new concept of her.

When a mentally handicapped child has to go into hospital, it is best to get advice on which hospital is attuned to his kind of problem. There are many handicaps. A doctor who knows how to make contact with mongol children may be nonplussed by his first encounter with an autistic child. If the family's general practitioner does not know of the right hospital with specialist knowledge for that child, the local branch of the National Society for Mentally Handicapped Children will probably be able to help.

Alternatively, advice can be sought from the societies that have been set up to look after the welfare of individual handicaps, e.g. the Spastics Society, the National Society for Autistic Children, and so forth. They will also advise on dentists and hospital dental departments with an active interest in handicapped children. This can be important, because many of them require a total anaesthetic for dental work of any complexity.

Next, Robin and Nicholas both had operations that were relatively straightforward, involving some but not too much discomfort. Nicholas came off slightly the worse with his secondary infection. But both were in a basically optimistic situation, in which the people around them would be radiating confidence rather than anxiety. The seriousness of a child's illness, and the worry that attends it, intensifies young children's problems in hospital, and makes the mother's role even more important.

Some children, even if they are very young, will have formed certain associations in their minds with hospitals and doctors. These may have visited somebody who was ill, and who later died. They may have registered the fear expressed by their parents about somebody who 'had to be taken to hospital'. This phrase is frequent enough and scarcely reassuring to a child with little experience of the world. Previous visits to an out-patients department may have been reasonably cheerful, or they may have been a bad preparation for a longer visit. Other children's comments about hospital can be very lurid, beyond any justification, as any nursery school teacher will confirm. All this can be damaging to the prospects of a young child going into hospital as an in-patient.

Children nowadays generally find themselves in children's wards. In general wards, they may be exposed to all manner of unpleasantness, unless they are placed with great care. This sometimes has to be arranged when overcrowding, or staff shortage, makes it unavoidable. In the case of long-stay children, paradoxically, there is a strong case, which is being argued now, for integration of children and adults in residential surroundings: this must reduce the unreality of a world that otherwise seems to be peopled only with children, nurses, teachers and visitors.

But it is clearly undesirable to allow children to observe at close quarters adults who are in considerable distress, or who are experiencing odd character changes as a result of drugs.

Cathy was eight when she had to go into a hospital near Belfast. 'I had to stay as still as possible for three days or so after an operation on a bone in my foot. So far as I could tell, there was no children's ward. I remember looking round this enormous room (it *seemed* enormous, at the time) and wondering who all these people were. In the next-door bed was an old man. He lay on his side, staring at me with huge eyes, but never saying a word. He must have had a terrible throat or chest trouble because he wheezed every so often. Soon after my operation I spilt some Ribena over my bed, and I couldn't move to do anything about it. I asked the man what I could do, but he said nothing. He just stared. That night I listened to him wheezing. It got worse and worse. I suppose I must have had a sleeping pill and I dropped off in the end. I woke up when I heard a grating sound, and saw a screen being put round the old man's bed. Somebody told me to go back to sleep. I don't know how, but I was absolutely certain, in a flash, that he had died. . . . I had nightmares about him for weeks.'

This kind of situation is rare now but not completely avoidable.

It will be remembered that when Robin was first admitted to his hospital he was taken off to the bathroom first thing. This is an interesting historical relic, dating back to the times when a bath was an important and unusual event for the majority of those entering hospital. At a time when the desirability of clean patients was just being appreciated, the importance of enforcing an admission bath seemed clear. Of course there are still children who are not very clean on entering hospital, but most mothers can and do try to see that their children are presentable, if not well scrubbed, before entry.

At Robin's hospital the procedure was more important than the care of the individual. This is one key difference between hospitals that means a great deal in the lives of the people who pass through them. Neither child needed a bath on entry. In Nicholas's case, this was observed. Later on, he would get one—

but only when he needed it, and when he was used to his surroundings.

Try to imagine what a four-year-old feels like when he is whisked away into a strange bathroom by a strange woman in uniform, without knowing what is going on and why his mother has been left behind. His clothes are then removed, and he is plunged into a bath. Strange hands—in most cases kind ones, but insistent ones—make sure he gets clean. A strange voice will be trying to distract him, to reassure him, and to express kindness. But meanwhile, psychologically, the child is being plundered of any individuality he may have. It can be a very bad start to a frightening experience.

Robin was not expecting his mother's disappearance when he returned from his bath. There is certainly no infallible way of preparing young children for the moment when they must realize that they have been left. The younger they are the less they will understand, let alone believe in the proposition that they are going to be left in hospital. Robin was given the basic idea, but this is not the same thing as appreciating how it feels when Mum, suddenly, is not there.

Nicholas was attended by his mother for a long time after entry. He got used to her going, and coming back after a brief period. By the time she disappeared for longer, Nicholas had got used to a particular nurse being especially concerned with him and what he was doing. There is no substitute for a long lead-in when a young child goes into hospital, before his mother leaves. When this cannot be managed for various family reasons it is all the more important for a nurse to be 'specialed' to him. At Nicholas's hospital, both these principles were accepted and applied. At Robin's hospital, it was customary to process the child into the standard system as soon as possible. This was not because the ward sister was callous—far from it. It was simply that she believed that in the best interests of everyone, the children's ward needed to be organized for optimum efficiency; this meant getting mothers out of the way so that nurses could do their jobs without interference, and so that the children could get the feel of hospital routine and begin to 'settle down'.

Nicholas's mother found that, with a few exceptions, she could enter into whatever was being done for her son. She could help with bathing, and changing the bedclothes, and she made herself useful, with other mothers, keeping the toy cupboard tidy and carrying away the trays of dirty plates and mugs after meals. Naturally, she kept out of the way of any nurses who were obviously in a hurry, and she was asked not to touch Nicholas's dressing after his operation. But the main point was that she felt she was part of a team who were helping Nicholas.

At Robin's hospital a mother was a visitor. If a mother showed any sign of wanting to do anything, she was quickly advised to 'leave it to nurse'. This can happen even in a ward which allows unrestricted visiting. Because it tends to reduce a mother's involvement with her child, it tends to hinder a child from acclimatizing naturally.

One of the encouraging trends in children's wards of the last few years is the increasing number who will put up a mother overnight. Some have found this very difficult to arrange, in buildings that were not planned with it in mind, but they have managed nonetheless. In Nicholas's case it meant that he had complete reassurance, knowing that his mother would be there throughout the important first night. Where Robin was, no such provision existed. His mother did not imagine that it was a reasonable request to make.

The 'pre-med' situation, just before an operation, can be a very alarming business. Some such experiences have been very graphically described in James Robertson's book *Hospitals and Children: a Parent's Eye View*. What happened to Robin at his pre-med is not recorded, but it would not be surprising if it approximated to some of the unhappier descriptions in that book. No young child is mentally equipped for sudden isolation, followed by the entry of a group wearing white masks. The injections and transportation by trolley can be macabre even if they are not really painful.

Nicholas's nurse told him about the pre-med well in advance. He was even allowed to put on a white mask himself, and observe the effect in a mirror. Here too the presence of his mother was very helpful.

Several hospitals that are very modern in the provision for child welfare in other respects draw the line at allowing a mother to be in attendance within a half day or a day after an operation itself. This is especially true of wards and hospitals dealing with ear, nose and throat cases. The argument centres on risk of infection. This is not a matter on which medical opinion is unanimous. There are several hospitals, such as Nicholas's hospital, where they set a higher store on having the mother close at hand at the moment when a child wakes up after an operation than on a theoretical gain in antiseptic conditions by excluding the mother for an arbitrary period. Waking up, dazed, weakened, and beginning to feel some discomfort, a child needs to perceive something that helps the world to seem natural again. This should be his mother.

When Robin's mother was allowed back for a visit, her son had already undergone the strange experience of regaining consciousness, and he may well have noted that he was still abandoned, *even then*. He next had a series of visits which were long enough to give hope that he might be back with his mother again; and brief enough to convince him that this was mere deception when she left. Length of time means very little to young children. Last year's summer holiday is often described as 'last week'. What they appreciate is what is happening *now*, and what is likely to happen in the near future. When mother starts to leave at the end of a visit, he ignores her 'only a few more days and I'll bring you back home'. What he reacts to is the return of abandonment. He loses control, cries and sometimes rages. This is why nurses often note that mother's visits are unsettling.

Gradually Robin seemed to adjust to hospital. He became quiet and even-tempered. This is appreciated in any hospital, for obvious reasons: because it is convenient, because it reduces disturbance to staff and to others, and also because it is medically desirable. But he was also adjusting *to his mother*, and *to other people*. He was forced to revise his relationships. Robin had to come to terms with a situation prematurely before experience could equip him for it. As a result, he lost his orientation: should he rely on his parents again? Should he ignore them, or treat them as incidental?

Should he punish them? Should he love them, and try to put the clock back? His disturbed behaviour at home, for months after his visit to hospital, showed very clearly how he vacillated between one attitude and another, while being unable to put his feelings into words.

Nicholas on the other hand did not need to adjust to anything more than hospital procedure, some new faces and a certain amount of pain. That is quite enough for a small boy. He coped with it, primarily because he felt he could rely on his mother's presence, and secondly because, in its dealings with him, his hospital was treating him as an individual who feels things. He was not simply another patient.

How typical are Robin and Nicholas?

A lot has been written in the past ten years about research into young children's hospital experiences. The basic message to be gained from clinical studies is that very young children (i.e. under the age of three) are very likely to be emotionally disturbed by going into hospital. At the age of three or four there is still a very high risk. From five onwards, the picture becomes progressively brighter, and disturbance can vary considerably according to the child's emotional maturity and his physical condition.

Some of the research follows up the children's reactions at home, some time after the event. This shows that the effects are often long lasting.

Up to five, then, most visits to hospital need to be regarded as involving very great risk, and steps must be taken to reduce that risk as far as possible. Clinical studies also demonstrate clearly that within this age range there is no real substitute for mother joining her child in hospital.

Robin and Nicholas then are fairly typical. Unfortunately, Robin is probably more typical than Nicholas, although the proportion of cases where mother and hospital together contrive to help a child avoid Robin's misfortunes is, happily, increasing. From five onwards, it will in most cases still be wisest for mother to go in with the child. Where the nature of the medical problem involves a lot of pain or discomfort, or where it leaves the child uncertain about what is going on (e.g. after concussion) the mother's presence becomes more important.

The older the child the more flexibility a mother can have in her arrangements to be near him. One recommendation made by perceptive nurses is that mothers who accompany older children into hospital should in most cases be more observant about their children's changing attitudes. Granted that constant attendance on the first day or two may be necessary, there comes a point where the child notices other children without their mothers, feels embarrassed, and wants to be like them. This does not mean that the child should be abandoned on the spot. It does mean that the time has arrived to avoid letting the child feel over-protected, and resentful.

Conducting research in this area is fraught with problems. Analysing the degree to which children can be said to be 'disturbed' is difficult enough, but comparing children's experiences between one hospital and another, and drawing conclusions about the importance of the mother entering hospital with the child, is unsatisfactory. Even if you show that the children accompanied by their mothers were better off, both during and after the event, anyone can claim: 'A lot of other influences could have biased the findings; for example, the nurses were different.' It is also possible to object that the children were different; their illnesses were different; their families were different; the overcrowding in the wards was different; and so on.

This makes it all the more impressive when a team of workers manages to prove beyond question that the mother's presence has a profound effect. This was achieved by D. J. Brain and Inga Maclay in 1968 in a study that came to be known as the Rubery Hill Report. They compared two groups of roughly a hundred children in each, who were all under six, all attending hospital for the first time, and all from similar backgrounds. Both groups were attending the same ward in the same hospital, and had identical operations—either for tonsils or adenoids, or both. The only difference between the groups was that in one of them the mother was not admitted with the child; in the other, the mother was admitted.

The results were highly significant. The children who had their mothers beside them suffered far less disturbance. Moreover, those children who had their mothers with them but could still be regarded as 'disturbed' (a minority in itself) proved to be better off than their counterparts in the motherless group *over time*. That is, they made a more rapid adjustment after returning home.

Perhaps the most significant point, however, is that an official independent committee, looking at all the evidence, reported in 1958 (The Platt Report) that the welfare of children in hospital demanded the presence of their mothers. It was adopted as official policy at Ministry level that provision should be made for mothers to have unrestricted visiting, at all reasonable times, and to be able to enter hospital with their children.

In 1972 official policy had not changed. If anything, the evidence had become even more convincing. A Ministry circular pointed out that the recommendations of the Platt Report had been carried out more slowly than was desirable for the good of children in hospital. It urged greater speed. This is why one is entirely justified in pressing the case for not separating young children in hospital. There is virtually no counter evidence—only habit.

At this point in time hospitals vary greatly in their attitudes and practice. In October 1971 the National Association for the Welfare of Children in Hospital (NAWCH) published the results of a survey of fifty-five hospitals in the London Metropolitan Region which regularly admit children as short-stay patients. Of these, thirty-one had no beds at all available for mothers who wanted to stay in with their children. A further ten provided them 'only in very special circumstances'. The rest had beds for use by mothers as a matter of course. The trend is towards this. But even in the last group there are differences between what should happen and what actually does happen.

Certain types of hospital are more restrictive than others. Isolation hospitals, dealing with serious communicable diseases, are an understandable case in point. Ear, nose and throat hospitals are another group which tends to be restrictive. (This makes the finding in the Rubery Hill Report, that children whose mothers stayed in hospital with them were no more likely to suffer post-operative infection, all the more pointed.)

To some extent, this is the result of difference in enthusiasm within hospitals themselves. But it is a fact that many mothers simply do not know about the possibility of staying in with their children; or, possibly, they do not feel it is necessary. A number of beds specially put into hospitals to take mothers have been under-used. Opinions differ on the main reasons for this. In some cases, ward sisters seem not to be at all keen to advertise these beds. Some mothers may be unable, for family reasons, to go in with their children. Others may want to do so but are too diffident to stake their claim.

All of these reasons probably hold good. The last one, however, may be particularly important. At the best of times, a hospital is an imposing institution. Even when the secretary and the medical staff smile, and are obviously friendly, it is impossible not to feel some awe in front of the system as such. It represents a feat of organization that commands respect. If, therefore, some-body at the hospital firmly suggests to a mother that her presence is really quite unnecessary, that person is perceived to be speaking not as an individual but with the whole weight of medical science embodied in the institution around her. 'They know best' (whoever they are) is perhaps a comforting philosophy. But unfortunately it often proves to be wrong.

Mothers, therefore, who let themselves be intimidated by the aura of the hospital into supposing that their fears about leaving their young children alone are unfounded, are partly contributing to delays in getting the Platt Report implemented. Obviously there are many other contributing factors—lack of money to re-structure group hospital wards being an important one—but this comparison between two mothers' experiences suggests that change ultimately depends on pressure from the public, quite as much as from the government.

Mrs T. and Mrs R.

Mrs T. and Mrs R. noticed each other in the waiting-room outside the children's ward at a local general hospital. Mrs R. was arriving with her three-year-old child just as Mrs T. was leaving. Mrs T.'s two-year-old had just been kissed good night, and told that mummy would be back next day. Mrs R., who had been alarmed by her doctor's insistence that her child should go into hospital for observation, noted Mrs T.'s worried look. There was a momentary exchange of sympathy in the glance they shared, which made it seem natural for them to talk to each other and compare notes in the days that followed.

Mrs R. was met by the ward sister, a large, middle-aged lady with authority in her deep voice. She had a welcoming smile and bent down instantly to greet the newly arrived toddler. For a time she went over with Mrs R. the documents she had received from the doctor.

'With children as young as this,' the sister explained kindly, 'we feel mothers should be allowed to come in at any time of the day. Let's say—between eight in the morning and eight at night. So feel free to drop in at any time.'

Mrs R. gulped. 'That sounds wonderful,' she murmured. Then, reaching for all the courage she had, she went on, 'As a matter of fact, I am very anxious to stay in with Sally overnight. Since she's been ill she's been waking at odd times, and—and I've read about how important it is to be with your child. I mean, she's only a toddler, and she hasn't the slightest idea what's going on. . . .'

The sister shook her head. She was polite, kind, but firm. 'That really isn't necessary, you know. A lot of fuss is made about children and hospitals. She may cry a bit, but she'll very soon get used to us. Stay around as long as you like, until Sally feels what the bed is like, and recognizes our faces.'

'I—I'm sorry, but I think I ought to stay in.'

The sister took her by the arm. 'I'm going to show you round the ward. You'll see how happy they all are.' She spoke quietly, with confidence that she would prevail.

Mrs R. was shown round the ward. Everything looked calm, correct, reassuring. The children in their beds certainly seemed to be comfortably 'settled-in'.

Just then there were screams from the corridor at the other end of the ward, easily audible through ths swing doors. The sister herself was surprised, and she turned back rather slowly, with Mrs R.

The disturbance came from Mrs T.'s child, who had been carried away from the ward to an adjoining room—partly because he needed changing and partly because his screams after separation were bad for morale. The nurse who was with him returned momentarily to the doorway, caught a look from the sister, and retreated in order to do a more thorough job of pacifying the child.

The sister nodded in the direction of the departing figure. 'It's often like that for a few minutes. Just like starting at school. He'll be just like the rest in no time at all.'

'I'm sure you're right,' replied Mrs R. But her resolve was hardening. Sally had a weak chest—how weak, and in what way had to be determined by tests—but her doctor had recommended taking precautions against her becoming over-tired or over-excited. It seemed medically inconsistent that Sally should be subjected to more emotional strain than was absolutely necessary. 'I must stay with her, you know,' she said quietly.

The sister switched her tactics to 'That is quite out of the question. It is against the hospital regulations, and I cannot——'

'I must,' Mrs R. persisted.

'But where on earth are you going to sleep?' The sister raised her voice, and smiled pityingly at Mrs R. as if she were temporarily out of her mind.

But she had presented Mrs R. with an opening. 'I'll just move that old armchair across, if I may. That will be quite enough for me.'

It is an interesting rule in life that a strong personality often finds he can only respect another strong personality. Once the sister realized how determined Mrs R. was she made the best of it. One of a set of separate cubicles (which had been kept empty in case a particular child who was an out-patient suddenly proved to need it) was put at Mrs R.'s disposal, together with one hospital bed and one camp-bed.

Mrs R. and Mrs T. met again in the ward soon afterwards, and frequently after that. They talked about their children, their problems, and the difference between the way their children took to the hospital. Mrs T. admitted later, 'I envied you your being able to stay in. I thought at first you must have special influence, or something. I just couldn't bring myself to ask.'

In this case, both children seemed to avoid really bad after-effects on their return home, possibly because Mrs T. was a very frequent visitor. But Mrs R.'s child was far less upset within the hospital itself, and co-operated much better as a patient. This is not just an example of what an individual can achieve. It is a reminder that systems or organizations do not change unless individuals make them change.

Nurses in the more liberal hospitals are sometimes critical of certain mothers even when they stay and visit. These criticisms are usually made of parents who stay in with their children but cannot imagine what to do. 'They meet up with each other and go out for coffee and a chat for longer than they talk to their children. They leave their kiddies in the cubicle for half the day, saying they'll be back in a few minutes. Those kiddies would be better off in an open ward, where they wouldn't just be left to themselves.'

Nurses also become aware of problems in a family when an anxious mother neglects her other children beyond reason in her efforts to be close to the hospitalized one. Social workers in hospital sometimes make a point of asking how a sick child's brothers and sisters are getting on—simply to draw attention to this point.

Sometimes parents seem obviously nonplussed. They feel they need to bring a present, which perhaps they can't afford. Or they say to the ward sister on the telephone, 'It's so late now! I can really only stay fifteen minutes. It's hardly worth it, is it?' But, in fact, few things are more worth it. Bringing a present isn't important. Nor, really, is staying a long time (except with young children at the beginning). What is vital is showing that you are keeping up the contact, and continuing to be a mother, a fixed point in an uncertain world.

Then again, there are parents who cannot face seeing their children ill, or talking to them about their illness. If this is their nature, they cannot be expected to change completely. But some effort in both directions can make a child much happier.

Summary of advice on short-stay hospitalization

These suggestions are prepared with the mother of a young child (below five years) in view. Some of them may not be entirely appropriate for older children, depending on their condition, and their emotional maturity. Here you must use your judgment.

A. PREPARATION

1 Find out now, before it becomes urgent, what the practice is at children's hospitals or children's wards near your home, with regard to unrestricted visiting, and mothers being allowed to stay in with young children. Your GP may know or the local branch of NAWCH, but there is no reason why you should not ask the hospital secretary direct. If you have brought your child to an out-patients' department, there is a strong likelihood that somebody there will discuss local practice with regard to in-patients. When your friends have taken children into local hospitals, ask them all about it, within the bounds of tact.

   This knowledge will guide you about the best place for your child to go into, other things being equal, should the need arise.

2 Prepare your child for hospital, in accordance with his age and understanding. Talk to him about hospitals, and what happens there. If you yourself had a bad experience in a hospital as a child, play it down in favour of a more optimistic picture. There are books that children may find helpful: three are mentioned in the References at the end of this book. But look through them carefully before buying, in case you feel your child may be unprepared for the detail.

3 Never give any false promises. By all means say that the doctors and nurses will help your child get better soon. But not tomorrow.

   Tell your child frankly about your own movements. 'I've

got to go home and see Richard now' may be greeted by tears, but will be regarded as honest, and fair, later. This is far better than saying 'I'll just be out for ten minutes,' when you mean, 'This afternoon, perhaps.'

Similarly, always say 'goodbye', if you are leaving. Never sidle out furtively.

4 Choose, with your child, something that is specially his, for him to take into hospital. Label it, if possible, and tell the nurse it belongs to him.

B. VISITING

1 If your child is between six months and five years, try to stay in with him, provided this is possible. Above five years —use your judgment about his emotional maturity and understanding. Staying in at the beginning is more important than what you do later.

2 Visit regularly and frequently, even if you are bored, don't know what to do, feel embarrassed, and aren't sure what to do with your child or talk about. Talk about ordinary things that are happening at home—what you all had for breakfast, etc. This all gives reassurance. But it is your presence that is as important as anything else.

3 If you have other children, they are bound to feel that some of your attention is being drawn away from them, towards the child in hospital. Avoid letting them feel they are losing all your attention, or that this state may be permanent.

4 Expect that there may be tears when you arrive to visit your child, and at your departure. This is normal. Absence of tears —if linked with disinterest—is not a good sign.

5 Try hard to come at the time you said you would come.

IN HOSPITAL

1 Ask questions when you do not understand something. The ward sister is invariably busy, and may look short-tempered: but nine times out of ten she will prefer to be asked questions (even the same question twice), rather than to see you become anxious and resentful through misunderstandings.

39

If you don't know what a 'drip' is exactly, or what 'in traction' means, don't be afraid to ask, because most mothers don't know either. Similarly, don't be afraid to telephone, at night, to find out how an operation went.

2 If your child is due for an operation, ask what steps are taken to prepare him for it. Be prepared to supplement yourself, if necessary: e.g. tell him the medical staff will wear white masks, if they won't tell him. Try to be with him close before and close after the operation, as far as is consistent with hospital practice.

3 There must be some basic rules, even in the most progressive hospitals. Respect them, if you have no sound reason for asking to bypass them. This is important, because it helps the long-term struggle to increase co-operation between parents and nursing staff, and get mothers accepted as desirable people.

By far the most frequently broken rule seems to be one that is fairly standard in children's wards. Sweets, biscuits, and so forth should be given to the nurses on the ward for distribution, and not brought in direct to a child in bed. If this rule is broken, important diets get disrupted; children eat chocolate on the sly, just before operations, and, which is downright cruel, diabetic children, or others that cannot enjoy sweets, are made to watch them being paraded in front of them. One ward sister protested to me that her staff were not customs officers: but they *had* to keep on the look-out, even to frisk some patients, to avoid the terrible sound of a caustic voice on the telephone—'Ops. Theatre here, sister. Young John Smith has just vomited under anaesthetic, and it looks like—yes, jelly babies. . . .'

Another important rule is to ask sister's advice about visiting if you have had contact with an infectious illness.

4 Try to make yourself useful in the ward: do the straightforward things that your child or his bed needs. But take care to do things *in the hospital way* (if there is one). And watch out for signs that your efforts may be resented by the nursing staff.

5 If, at any time, it seems possible and reasonable that a young child should be brought back home to continue his treatment in bed there, even though he is not fully recovered, do not hesitate to broach the subject, but obviously you must follow medical advice.

6 Remember that the medical staff are human. They feel success, failure, enthusiasm, frustration. When a particular case seems to defy medical experience and treatment, they are sympathetic but they become more tense, more irritable and less communicative. This can affect the atmosphere in a whole ward. Invariably, parents are concerned almost exclusively about their own child. It is easy to forget that the staff may need to concentrate more attention on somebody quite different.

AFTERWARDS

Expect some trouble: or, at least, don't be surprised if it comes. However well organized everything has been for the welfare of your child, he may go through a period of feeding problems, rudeness, and tantrums, and he may seem to have forgotten many of the things he had learnt before. You and your child may be lucky. But there is often a reaction to hospital. You can help it to be a short one by keeping a lot of contact with him after his return; and trying to be as fair as you can, complimenting him when he does something well, and stopping him when he's naughty, to emphasize that your family relations and standards are what they always were. He will appreciate your giving his world a 'normal structure' after the impact of going away from home.

Four
Long-term Stay in Hospital

After three months in hospital, the Department of Health and Social Security classifies a child as 'medium-stay'; after two years, 'long-stay'. In practice nobody is certain in many cases just how long a child will be in hospital if he is suffering from something more serious then a broken leg, although in other cases where handicap is very severe, a child may be put into hospital with the conscious intention that he should stay there (or in a similar institution) permanently. But there is little point in this book in distinguishing between medium- and long-stay. The problems of each of these are very similar for the child.

There are various reasons why some children have to spend a long time in hospital. In only a minority of cases do the parents have much choice in the matter, but they have a longer period of time, in most cases, to look around at different hospitals and at specialized individual units, both before entry, and after entry if they are disquieted.

It is convenient to distinguish between children who are hospitalized for physical reasons and for mental handicaps or mental illness. In fact, there is a lot of overlap. Indeed, one of the tragedies of long stay in hospital for physical reasons is the possibility that a form of mental handicap may overtake the child. This is the measure of the need for improvement of care for long-stay children in this country.

A child who is dependent on medical attention at a moment's notice may need to be in hospital. It is arguable whether any of the others really do, provided an adequate alternative is possible. Unfortunately, it very often isn't. A child born without arms as a result of thalidomide is not, strictly speaking, ill. Yet some such children are in hospital and others are not. If there were sufficient specialist residential schools, and if all parents with handicapped children were able to cope with looking after them during weekends and holiday periods, long-stay wards might be stripped of most of their occupants overnight.

Long stay in a hospital is being committed to an utterly unreal world. This world may be a safe, healthy, kindly one, but it will be one which is missing most of the stimulation we take for granted. A child who spends his formative years in this situation cannot develop any kind of realistic understanding of how the outside world, or how normal human relationships, are meant to work. This is generally recognized nowadays. There is a horrifying gap, however, between recognition and correction of a thoroughly bad situation. It is official policy to phase out children's long-stay in hospitals in favour of residential centres where children stand a chance of reasonable education and of meeting ordinary people, not just other child patients and medical staff. This is the intention, but it will take time.

Meanwhile, what are parents to do, with more than one child, with inadequate housing, without help from relatives, and perhaps with a marriage drifting closer to the rocks, when they find they cannot continue looking after a severely handicapped child at home? Even if they have plenty of money they will find long waiting lists at private schools or homes that would be otherwise prepared to take the child. They could hire a nanny, although very little of the cost is likely to be paid back by the State. Remembering Helen Keller (the blind, deaf and dumb girl who was educated and given a meaningful life by a nurse of great courage and perseverance), they might favous this. But nurses like Helen Keller are rare indeed, and while this is a situation that preserves home life it is also a form of unreality—without other children, without going to school, and all the experiences that they can bring.

Many such parents, unable to find anything better by themselves, and told by a local authority that there is no viable alternative, will settle for a kind of hospitalization. They may regret the decision. It is so close to the emotive expression 'putting him away'. But they will tell themselves that they owe it to each other, and to the rest of their family. They are possibly right, in that it cannot help a handicapped child to be held responsible for a family breakdown, in a way he can never properly understand.

This is a preamble to another comparison, this time between what can go wrong with a long-stay patient, and what can happen in the best circumstances to alleviate the problems.

Derek

Derek was a perfectly normal, healthy little boy. He was bright for his age. At three he had a wide vocabulary. He could follow stories on television very capably, and he liked building complex interlinking garages for his toy cars. Then, a real car ran over him.

About, say, fifteen years previously, it is highly doubtful whether Derek would have survived. As it was, a highly skilled medical team managed to save his life. As this happens more and more often nowadays, more children with permanent multiple injuries are likely to need special provision—as did Derek.

Part of his rib cage had to be artificially reconstructed. Although he eventually regained some control over his leg muscles, he has been unable to walk. Strain on his heart has been something that everyone has had to guard against. Being virtually without bladder control, needing consistent aid with feeding, and requiring a very careful guard against the possiblity of infection, he obviously presented very considerable problems for anybody who was to look after him. His parents, with two other children, could hardly be blamed for balking at the idea that he might be brought home. This idea was only briefly mooted, in fact.

One thing was uncertain at this time. Derek had been unconscious a long while, looked dazed, was under drugs a lot, and found that saying anything was both tiring and painful. He had no obvious brain damage, but in this situation it was hard to be certain. Had anyone been certain it would obviously have affected what could be expected of him in the future. The best signs were that he was regaining a sense of fun, and he clearly enjoyed listening to his mother.

Derek was transferred to a children's hospital that took long-stay patients five months after his accident. The hospital was a long way from his parents' home. His mother was apprehensive about being able to visit him as often as she should. It was already very difficult for his father—whose work took him away from home—to see him more than about once a month.

At first Derek was in a cubicle by himself. By the time he was four and a half, he was felt to be sturdy enough to move into a small ward with seven other children, of varying ages and disabilities. Two of these were mobile, with the aid of wheel-chairs. The rest were incapable of much movement and had little communication with each other except for one older boy called Michael, who was intelligent, and dying of muscular dystrophy. Michael had great curiosity and tried to make contact with each of the other children, as far as he could.

It may seem odd that Derek should have been put into these surroundings in order to begin the long climb back towards normal development, but by this time Derek's parents had learnt that there is very little choice in these matters. In any case, what exactly are the right surroundings? Derek had to be under very close medical surveillance for a year after his accident. He could not have stood up to rough-and-tumbles with other boys, so that being with normal children would have been dangerous. He was below school age, so there was no formal education to demand. The ward was cramped, but attractive and run on very efficient lines.

For a long time Derek's mother was encouraged by Derek's progress. He learned to use his voice again without pain. He moved about more in bed, and could manœuvre a pillow and a wedge under his shoulders so that he could sit up. Every time she visited, which was once every week when she could manage it, Derek's mother felt that he was getting stronger, and the questions he asked reflected more of the eager interest in life that he had shown as a toddler.

Then her view suddenly changed. It dawned on her that after a time a limit was reached in what was being done. An enormous proportion of Derek's day was spent waiting for things to happen, and being part of regular routines. Michael had a transistor, which the nurses turned on to Radio 1 to provide a diverting background to the bed-pan ritual, the inspections for bed-sores, and the washing with flannels. There seemed to be different nurses in the ward every few weeks. Partly for this reason they tended to go by numbers in identifying the children's equipment and possessions, and even, sometimes, in referring to the children themselves. There was the occasional nurse that Derek liked, and talked to, but she was soon gone.

Derek's mother understood that there was a room that was used as a classroom by older, more mobile children, in another part of the hospital, and that there was a visiting teacher for them. But when she asked, she was told that there was no question of the teacher visiting the wards themselves, or of providing any kind of nursery-school activities. It was a nice idea, the matron agreed: but quite impracticable.

There was some exciting progress being made. A physiotherapist was getting Derek used to sitting in a wheel-chair. This was a slow business, and could only be for short periods.

'We need to concentrate on getting him well,' said the matron. Her tone was sympathetic, but the remark was pointed.

Derek's mother could not help making comparisons between him and her other children from a mental point of view. In simplest terms, they developed, but he did not. He picked up new words, and learned to do some difficult jigsaws. Talking with Michael, he learned lots about policemen and burglars, and rockets to the moon. But when Michael was taken away, she realized suddenly what a great source of help had been there by accident, and was now gone.

There was something strange about Derek's personality too. It was not very surprising perhaps that he should have stopped asking questions about his father, and why he never came to visit. After all, his father had only visited him seven times in all. (Now he was divorced, and released from the obligation.) But Michael's disappearance could have been expected to have meant more to him. Instead, Derek complained, rather petulantly, about a picture book of cars that he claimed Michael had promised him. He asked no questions about Michael. He had no strong feelings about people, his mother concluded, except for what they might provide.

As six, Derek's life underwent a considerable change. The accident insurance question was at last settled and his mother was allowed to invest the money to guarantee him a qualified home nurse for life. By this time he could use a wheel-chair for part of the day, and was thought by the doctors at his hospital to be a safe risk to be allowed home. He is taught at home by a home tutor provided by his local education authority: later, if all goes well he may be able to attend a State school for delicate children, with special transport provided.

He is now seven. He is babyish in many ways that make him different from his brothers. Despite being used to only weekly visits from his mother in the past, he now has very great alarm when his mother is out of the house for long. If she talks to his brothers, he immediately competes with them for attention. He is agreeable enough to the idea of learning things, but he has very poor concentration and finds it hard to remember anything from one lesson to another. His tantrums and his baby language suggest that he really wants to be treated like a baby again. When he is taken outside it is usually into a small courtyard at the back of the house, or through some back streets to a recreation ground. Other places, particularly where there are lots of cars and people, seem to frighten him.

He is adjusting to home life, but gradually. It might almost be asked, wasn't he better off in hospital, where at least he was placid? But being placid cannot be all there is to life. If a child 'settles down' after a while in hospital, and is predictable in his reactions and behaviour, he is obviously less of a nuisance from an administrative point of view and easier to care for medically. It is even possible to argue that he is content, and therefore happy. But this is tantamount to saying that keeping somebody alive, well, clean, adequately fed and comfortable is sufficient, without bothering about mental needs. The contrary view, that life in a compartment is both a waste and unfair, involves difficulties of planning, and (as in Derek's case) a considerable wrench when reality is substituted for a compartment. Adjustment to reality is difficult, takes time, but (if medical demands allow) it must be worth it, provided human relationships are valued.

But there are other hospitals which seem to make significantly better attempts to provide for the mental, as well as the physical, care of long-stay children.

Betty

Betty is at one of these. She is now ten, and has spent half of her life in a small hospital situated in the countryside. This building was used as an isolation hospital in Victorian times. More recently it has been used for children with a variety of different illnesses, and for some with mental handicap. It is slightly unusual in having a very close relationship with a neighbouring church, and the C of E school attached to that. For some time now, the tradition has been established that the church and its school involve themselves, via the Friends of ———— Hospital organization, in developments that could aid the welfare of the children in the hospital.

They see to it, for example, that those children who do not receive visits, and who bear the signs of having been 'dumped', are given attention, are brought into outings, and do not miss out on birthday treats or at Christmas time. The play group leader organizes kindergarten activities both inside the hospital and (on certain mornings) for local non-hospital children in the church hall.

Betty has been partly paralysed since an attack of polio. Like Derek, she took some considerable time before being able to move about in a wheel-chair. Now, however, she is skilful—even daring—when she rides around.

Whereas Derek was attended by a succession of nurses, none of whom meant anything very special to him, Betty was under the close attention of two people from the moment she was admitted. One of these was a staff nurse who had charge over a 'family group' of six children. The other was a young social worker. The nurse had Betty as one of her 'cases': this meant getting to know Betty well, finding out what she was interested in, talking to her a lot, making it obvious that she was concerned for her comfort, administering a certain amount of kindly discipline, making sure she was getting the best out of the play and education facilities that were laid on—all this, and more besides. She did not simply see her job as one of making sure that Betty was clean, well fed, and well provided for medically. She was much more of a mother substitute. This was just as well, because Betty's mother has not been near her daughter for nearly four years.

It may seem impossible for a staff nurse to contrive to do so much—not just for Betty, but for five other children as well. Two key elements are important here. First, the social worker, the play group leader (and the other teachers for that matter), and the medical staff all co-operate and collaborate. They get together and discuss particular children's ups and downs. This may sound elementary, but it is by no means routine in all hospitals for people with different training, and with different jobs to do. For example, in other hospitals:

Matron

'The last visiting teacher left about a month ago. Another one's supposed to be coming, but I still don't know when. Frankly, we can all do without one for a bit. It's obviously right that the older ones should get some teaching. And reading, writing, and doing sums doesn't make much of a mess. But the last one had ideas about free expression—you know, making things out of bits of clay. . . . I don't know what that's supposed to teach them. The spastic children can't manage it at all. It makes a terrible mess everywhere, and we get late for this, and late for that. . . .'

Teacher

'I don't mind having to improvise things, and I don't have too many wrangles with the nurses. Two things I do regret. The first is that when children are working on a project— like making an airport, or a model village—if they're really interested they don't want to leave it just to the hour or so when I can get them into the classroom. But all the equipment has to be kept religiously outside the ward. The other thing is talking to the consultant, or the registrar. I won't say the time-table is organized so that I can never see them, but it works out that way. You see sometimes a child will talk to me—about losing something, about being afraid of the other children, about visits he's not getting—when I'm quite sure he says nothing to the nurses. I'm sure that sometimes knowing what is going on in a child's mind must help. But if I talk to the nurses about anything like that, they either smile or they shrug their shoulders.'

So Betty was lucky in her hospital.

Educationally, she is about average—neither brilliant in any way, nor lagging behind. Her best subject is probably English. She reads clearly, with a lot of expression. (Many children who have been in hospital a long time, and who can read, either lack expression or reserve it for blood and thunder situations where the need for it is obvious: their reading ability has advanced beyond their understanding. She has problems over getting her writing to be faster and smaller since she has to guide her pencil with both hands. But she is working on it. Most sensibly, her teacher gives her large art blocks (about 2 feet square) to write on, and they are supported on a simple wooden frame that fits on her bedside table-tray, which was made as a workshop project by an older child.

Betty has a strong imagination, and she is encouraged to use it. Despite not knowing much about what happens outside a hospital, she is not in the least deterred from hazarding guesses in her drawings and in her writing. She had heard of school desks, but had never been in an ordinary classroom: she produced a splendid drawing of a class in which each child sat working at a directorial desk. The teacher wore a light blue coat, as her own teacher usually did. But the children were all dressed in a magnificent mixture of fashions and colours. The girls wore frocks, trouser suits, gowns, riding-gear—all in bright colours. The boys were in the football shorts and jerseys she had admired on television.

The teacher's skill lay not in pointing out where Betty was wrong or unrealistic. It was in indicating to her gradually and tactfully what there was outside, and how it all fitted together, without stifling any of her imaginative, exploratory urge.

Betty seemed to have a very good balance between self-sufficiency—wanting to get on with something that interested her—and asking questions from other people. She concentrated hard on what she did, and took both a pride and a pleasure in it.

Of course she had difficult times. Occasionally she would feel very frustrated—at running out of paper, or not being able to grasp something properly, at things not turning out as she wanted. Then she would bawl, and argue with other children, especially one girl, with whom she competed for attention from her 'special' nurse. She could be naughty too. Once she played up the social worker by pretending to have lost all use of her arms, and later (when the social worker's back was turned) seizing her notes and tucking them under her mattress.

But there can be few children who do not do this at home. This is what makes Betty's whole personality seem surprisingly normal and un-institutional. Not for her the mouselike acceptance of monotonous well-disciplined routine that is the true mark of the institutional child. It seems a shame that her parents don't seem to want to come and admire her.

The differences between Derek's and Betty's hospitals run very deep. Apart from some obvious variations in personality and outlook of the staff immediately concerned with the wards, there are the questions of the hospital traditions; of the attitude and involvement of the consultant paediatricians; of the chain of command in each hospital; of the relative turnover in staff. All these can, in their way, affect what happens to the individual child in the ward.

And yet the staff at Derek's hospital very likely had the best possible of intentions with regard to caring for their children. It is difficult to blame them if their concept of care, derived from their training, is largely physical. 'They do very well here,' one matron once told me with some pride, 'when you think of poor people outside, or how they used to suffer in the old days.' She was right. The children in her ward were warm, comfortable, clean and observed carefully for any change in their physical condition. But comparing their mental state, and what they had to look forward to, with normal children of our present time, was simply not part of her outlook.

Derek and Betty were just two children. But it does not take much research, by way of visiting hospitals and other residential units, to see that there are a painfully large number of children who show the signs of the development that was beginning to affect Derek; and to see that Betty is one of painfully few children who seem, somehow, to have avoided this Long-Stay Personality.

There are a number of traits that make up Long-Stay Personality, which may appear in a range of different combinations in different children. The clearest way to describe these is to present, briefly, some more children who have spent too long a time being mentally undernourished:

Bill is five, and has never known close contact with an adult since he was about eighteen months old. He is an attention-hunter, but when he has got an adult's attention, he does not know what to do with it. He gets frustrated, bad-tempered, whines for sweets, and is rude. If he sees you for the first time in the ward, he shouts 'Hey, mister! Come over here.' You smile, cross over, and try to talk to him about what he is doing. He cannot converse, however, apart from the simplest question-and-answer basis. His basic understanding of adults is that they provide food, clothes, and a time-table on which they insist. If he is lucky, they give him sweets. There is nothing now which could be said to be wrong with him physically (except for an allergy) or mentally. And yet the first teacher to talk to him has commented that he is going to need a lot of help if he is to get anywhere educationally. (At his age she is avoiding saying 'sub-normal', but it is obvious that that is in her mind.) Bill competes for attention (which in itself is good) but in a way that makes him pugnacious with other children, and unpopular. He has fits of jealous rage, in which he may seize and break every toy within range.

The future is going to be difficult for him, and for the community that will need to draw him into its orbit.

Shirley is seven, and uses a wheel-chair. For some time, after her mother disappeared and her father died, she used to be visited regularly by her grandmother. By all accounts, Shirley used to benefit considerably from this, and seemed a bright four-year-old, but for the last three years this grandmother has been in a geriatric ward.

Shirley is very shy of new faces. She puts her hands across her eyes and peeps out at them between her fingers. The nurse in her ward is a recent arrival, and she reports that Shirley is the same with most people. It was very difficult for the nurse, who is the kind who really wants to, to make close contact. Shirley seems to be deeply suspicious of other people. When they say they are coming back she reserves her judgment. She discounts any suggestions or promises that belong to the future.

Like Bill, she has poor concentration, and is forever picking up or changing objects to play with, or to put in her mouth and suck. It is difficult to tell how much she understands when you talk to her. She has little concept of the outside world, beyond the hospital gates: talking about shops, or towns, or farms, seems to leave a similar kind of impression on her that a talk about fairies or Martians might. This may be partly due to lack of opportunity to see things; cars, for example, she *does* believe in, and talks about, because she has seen them in the hospital car park, and has ridden several times in a minibus. But it is likely that her distrust of people is hindering her as well. On the few occasions that she has been taken outside the hospital she gave signs of being very frightened by the noise, and by the general strangeness.

John, at thirteen, seems a good deal younger than he really is. He has had bronchial trouble on and off for years: serious enough to be looked after carefully, but not so serious that he would have had to stay so long in a hospital and later a residential school for delicate children had not his mother, or the rest of his family, been incapable of looking after him at home.

His vocabulary is very limited, and he likes slipping into a babyish voice and tone every so often. He seems quite disinterested in most things, once he has sampled them for a few minutes. Typically, he will insist on being allowed towards the front of a group watching television; then he will get bored, provoking arguments and fights with the children he is disturbing.

His behaviour is by no means always unpleasant, however. He can be friendly enough in conversation. But usually he hints in his manner that he is not so much interested in sharing ideas, or finding out, or making contact, as in fishing for some kind of present or advantage. He does not make friends, only acquaintances.

Apparently he had been, over a period of a year, particularly attached to a young woman who helped in the dormitory at his residential school. They got on very well together, and it was a considerable blow to him when she married and moved to the North of England. This needs to be understood in conjunction with the fact that prior to this John had spent a little time on a 'trial run' with his uncle and aunt, and it became clear that this arrangement was not going to work. It must be difficult for a child in this situation not to feel he has been rejected, or let down, several times over—starting with his parents.

Something he has done which other observers have noticed in separated children is to develop a complex story in his mind about his real family. This is important to him, and he transmits small extracts from it to impress his teacher only when he wants to be both friendly and impressive towards her. This fantasy makes his mother out to be a television actress, who is so busy with her commitments that she cannot spare the time to be with him. His dependence on the television set is thought by his teacher to be connected with a desire to see somebody he can claim as his mother on the screen. This may be a bit fanciful, but he has had to substitute a lot of fantasy for reality in his thoughts and his outlook to a degree at which it is difficult for him to develop normal relations with people, or to meet new faces and opportunities objectively.

*   *   *

Naturally, children are individuals and they react to their circumstances individually, but the kind of reactions that they are liable to have after a prolonged stay in a hospital, or anywhere for that matter where they are cut off from being part of a family, can be seen reflected in Bill, Shirley and John. While each of them has some individual features in history and make-up, they all show, to some extent or other, common traces of Long-Stay Personality. These can be summed up as:

Being at a distance from reality; finding it difficult to understand what is real and what is talked about or on television; not making friends easily; being prone to arguments and squabbles, rather than to co-operating with adults or with each other; being acquisitive, anxious to grab for anything that is going; being more determined not to be let down by anyone than to help anyone; callousness towards others, and lack of interest in them or concern for their property. Attention-seeking but suspicious of friendly approaches, or promises of future contact and help. Lack of concentration; restricted interest in learning (of many kinds); low imaginative response, except in personal fantasies, which can sometimes be dominant. According to circumstances, there may be more sense of loss; of being a second-class, under-privileged child; or over-dependence on a particular link with somebody, with no fall-back position if the link is broken.[1]

This is painting the picture at its worst. It can be far better, as in Betty's case. But for all children separated in this way the danger exists. Those who have a parent to make regular contact, and to press for improvements in their surroundings and their welfare, have a better chance of avoiding the danger.

A parent without much money, with poor health, or with many other responsibilities may sometimes feel powerless to help. Once he realizes that his child is being handicapped by the static state of his compartment, to an uncertain degree—possibly even as much as the handicap that put him into hospital—he sees, or senses, various alternatives:

[1] In other countries, too, something akin to Long-Stay Personality has been found —as in Geiger's study of children provided for by the State in Russia, in 1966.

a Protest—possibly effective, but limited.
b Bringing child home.
c Seeking removal to another hospital or a community home.
d Investigating the possibility of fostering.
e Despair.

Nobody is more aware of the bad effects of a long hospital stay on children in institutional conditions than the Department of Health and Social Security. Various policies and recommendations bear witness to this. The progressive phasing out of large, institutional children's hospitals in favour of residential homes, which should be homes first and hospitals second, is particularly important for the future. But it takes time and money: and both parents and children have problems which are urgent now.

There is similar promise in the 1971 Education Act, which extends the responsibility of the Department of Education and Science to providing for the schooling of all handicapped children. But the Department cannot tell local authorities overnight what to set up to cope with local special education problems, nor can it help them to implant this immediately into wards that are caring for the body almost to the exclusion of the mind.

Meanwhile, a parent has to pick and choose. If he is to do the best for his hospitalized child, he has to try to bend the odds in favour of his child. Maureen Oswin in her book The Empty Hours shows clearly that whether a long-stay child is to be regarded as a human being, who must develop, or simply as a case, which needs to be looked after, is very much a matter of chance. 'It is the variations in care,' she claims, 'that are so shameful.' We are well into the 1970s, yet there are enormous differences in the attitudes and practices of hospitals that are progressive, and have the people who can effect changes and make them work, and those which are (slightly) updated versions of the old Poor Law workhouses; there are differences between local authorities in the extent to which they are prepared to see long-stay cases as an urgent problem that they should be helping to solve; and there are differences between wards, and between dormitories in residential homes and schools, depending on differences between staff.

In this situation, what can a parent do? Here are some suggested guide-lines.

1 The most important thing to preserve, for a young child, is a strong link with home and family. Ideally, he should be looked after at home: this may be impossible, but the possibility should be regularly and objectively reviewed.

2 Any system of partial boarding should be the next best solution. Again, if this is not possible at once it might be well worth considering later. With many residential schools for handicapped children it is common practice to have weekly boarding. But many hospitals are prepared to make arrangements of this kind nowadays.

3 Wherever a child is, if he is away from home, there must be regularity of contact. He may not react exactly as you might wish when you visit him. He may not, even, seem to notice the visit. But he will certainly notice failure to visit. His reactions to this are at the core of the development of Long-Stay Personality.

   Financial help is available from the State to those of limited means who have a long way to go to visit their children in a hospital or a home. The nearest Citizens' Advice Bureau, or office of the Department of Health and Social Security, can be consulted about this.

4 If your child has an unusual and very special illness, there may be little or no choice about where he goes to hospital. Even so, some choice may be possible, in the sense that he may be able to be transferred after a time. If you have any degree of choice, have a very good look at alternatives, before committing your child to a hospital, a home or a school.

5 When looking at alternatives, remember what are bad signs and what are good signs.

a *Bad signs*
   Too much bare wall, tidiness, silence—all portents of coldness and clinical efficiency.

   The complete opposite—total disorganization, dirt, fighting

unchecked, etc. (This is perhaps uncommon, but not rare).

Lack of evidence of spontaneity and warmth between members of the staff and the children.

Lack of occupation for the children.

Absence of toys; toy cupboard locked during the daytime.

No, or very little, personalization of children's bedside areas: do they have their own pictures up? their own cupboards, or cubby-holes? bedside rugs? etc. No evidence that children have the opportunity of some privacy—e.g. in the loo.

Signs of Long-Stay Personality among the children: are they attention-hunters? do they have poor concentration? do they bicker and fight, instead of playing together?

A rota preventing continued contact between particular staff and a particular set of children.

b *Good signs*

A sense of fun and alertness among the children.

Interior designs that seem to have been adapted to make the place more like a real home, less like a hospital, and more like a place where children change the decorations.

Particular staff providing special care for particular children; rota arranged for maximum individual care.

Staff stopping to talk with children, as opposed to talking to children.

Arrangements made even for severely handicapped children to be taken outdoors on warm, sunny days.

Evidence of frequent outings, trips. (N.B. A fortnightly visit to see houses, shops, traffic, etc., is a far better sign than an annual trip to the seaside.)

Evidence of time-tables being adapted (but not disrupted) to individual children's interests, as well as their needs.

Models, paintings, hobbies, etc., being treated as serious and worth displaying and taking notice of by the staff.

Five
Family Break-up
I: General

'Staying together for the children's sake' is a very old concept. When a man and his wife no longer want to live with each other, they often see themselves faced with a difficult choice. This is between patching up differences and trying to make continuation of the marriage as little unpleasant as possible, so as to protect the interests of their young children, or splitting up in order that each should get the most out of life while accepting the risk of this action to their children's happiness.

There is a different kind of question, however, which other people sometimes ask themselves: is it in fact better for the child to endure living with estranged parents, or to cut the losses and risk the effect of the split on their children in order to stop them living in an unhappy home?

This second question is a more modern one to ask. Clearly, the way it is put is tilting the likely response in the direction of separation or divorce on these lines: 'You know you and your wife cannot change your real natures, so accept the idea that it is better for everyone if you split up.'

This point is more easily made today when divorce carries relatively little social stigma; and when it is realized that a child of divorced parents is unlikely to be the only one at his school, and will therefore be less vulnerable on the subject than, say, forty years ago.

There are also quite a number of people who refer back to their childhood in these terms:

'I used to hate being in the house at week-ends; and I never wanted to have my friends visiting me, in case my parents started quarrelling again. Just when you thought everything was quiet, and you could say to yourself, "This week, anyway, they seem more cheerful", my mother would suddenly make a remark that showed how bitter she was underneath. When I was fifteen they each told me, separately, that they were going to live apart from now on, and they would be getting a divorce. My father was very shy, as if it was still too early for me to be exposed to this kind of thing. But I couldn't help thinking how much happier we might have been if they had gone ahead and done it years before that.' (S.P., a successful businessman aged thirty-five. Married; two children.)

'Daddy drank rather heavily. For days, maybe a week or two on end, he used to be kind, friendly, and easy to get on with. Then he'd come back late, say three nights in a row, and he'd wake me up and insist on reading me stories. The day after he'd be terrible: he could suddenly turn very strict and tell me off for not cleaning my shoes before breakfast. It would sound like a joke, but he was deadly serious. . . . Sometimes my mother took me down to my grandmother's for a few days, and she'd tell me (i.e. grandmother) that daddy was having a difficult time at his office, and that every-thing would be better soon. Then I'd be brought back home, and everything would be fine—for a week or so. In the end, almost as soon as I'd taken my "O" levels, Mummy told me that she was definitely splitting up. I must have shown her how delighted I was, because she seemed rather shocked. I only wished it had happened long before.' (J.G., twenty-eight. She is a journalist. Twice married.)

In 1966, Landis published research which showed that many older children, particularly if they felt they had been 'used' by either party, expressed relief at the parents' divorce.

This kind of reminiscence is not uncommon. At the same time, it is not typical; and does not necessarily reveal the complete truth. It is tempting to accept young adults' descriptions of their feelings, when they seem confident, independent, realistic and modern in outlook, at face value. But everyone likes to think they are ahead of their parents, in some way. Where a marriage was patched up for their sakes, an obvious outlet for the children's resentment later on is derision of their parents' archaic attitudes. They are inclined, therefore, to exaggerate the degree to which they would have preferred their parents to have split up; and in looking back to ascribe greater perception and strength of mind to themselves as children than they really possessed.

On the other side of the picture, there is this comment by a matron who looks after the junior boarders at a girls' boarding-school.

'A number of them have parents who have broken up. A few seem fairly thick-skinned about it. But I can tell that it affects most of them a lot. Take Sandra, for instance. She is eight, and she boards during the week. Practically all the time she's actually here she enjoys herself. She's very outgoing, and she's popular with the others. She has a good sense of humour, and always gets us laughing. Friday evening, though, she goes off again—usually with her mother, sometimes with her father. I imagine they're very nice with her. But on Monday morning she's so miserable! When she decided she could talk to me about it, she wailed, 'I don't want to go with just Daddy, or just Mummy; I want to be living all together again with both of them.' Her parents have in fact been separated now for over two years, so it's obviously been quite painful to her, for a long time.'

What is clear, however, are these points:

a In certain circumstances, parents prolong the married state, with their children at home, to the disadvantage of those children.

b Parents sometimes overestimate, as well as underestimate, the degrees to which their children need and expect both their parents to be living together happily with them.

Since we are in an age where both these points are likely to be made more of, rather than ignored, it is important from the children's point of view to try to set some limits to them.

First, it is obvious that some parents conceal their differences, and their incompatibility, more successfully than others. There are those who reserve their arguments for times when the children are out of earshot; who arrange to do things with their children, separately, or together when they are both feeling like it; who prepare convincing reasons for their separate holidays. Possibly, even, they are strong-minded about not trying to influence their children against each other. These parents are unlikely to deceive a child completely, but they can certainly keep their home a pleasant and stable environment in which he can be brought up.

At the other extreme are cases—such as the home of J.G., described above—where one or even both parents appear to be having a particularly bad influence on the child. Where one of them is violent, takes drugs, or acts vindictively towards their child, there is a strong argument for splitting the home to benefit the child.

Between these two ends of the spectrum there are a large number of possible types of family. It is here that making decisions about what is best for the child becomes really difficult.

When there is a child below five, there should, if possible, be a mother. This basic point comes straight out of all the preceding parts of this book.

Up to five, there is desperately little understanding of adults' ideas and feelings. If there is a break-up and the mother leaves, it is all too easy for the child to relate all the details to himself—e.g. 'She doesn't love me. There must be something about me that she doesn't love'; or, 'Maybe it was me being naughty that sent her away'; or, occasionally, 'X took her away from me', and the variation 'Daddy sent her away from me'. All these motives can be detected among young children, and among many who are not so young—who were separated from their mother when the family broke up. They are nagging ideas, which can affect their character and outlook in later life. It is rather like having a bad examination result the very first time your knowledge of a subject is put to a test: this can colour your attitudes to the subject as a whole, to examiners, to examinations, to your own skill. . . .

The task of a second woman who takes over as mother is by no means impossible when a child is as young as this. That would be the last thing to suggest. But it is not easy to form a close relationship that will supply most of what has been taken away.

The same applies to the task of a father bringing up a young child without its mother in the house. He has more to do than simply restore a feeling that the home is secure, and that his child will not find himself entirely alone; he has to make frequent, warm contact with his child, encouraging hugs, questions, requests to read and join in games. It is a tall order for somebody who has to go out to work.

This is not just because the under-five doesn't understand. If his first reliance on love and attachment is shown to be misplaced, because suddenly his mother is no longer there, his framework for building other relationships is left in a faulty condition. Some examples of this are given below.

If his father leaves, of course that matters too. But in all probability it will mean considerably less, under five, than to be without mother. This is partly because fathers are much less often in evidence round the house; because fathers are not seen to be responsible for warmth, food, comfort, allaying fears, and so on; and because fathers are less demonstrative of affection, and are sometimes shy, or friendly rather than loving.

When a mother has a profound reaction against the role of housewife and mother, and is away, unpredictably, for long periods, reliance can be transferred to the father, or even to somebody else in the family. But these are exceptional circumstances. By and large, the important constant factor in a child's life should be his mother.

Only in unusual cases does it seem justifiable to deny a young child either of his parents, or to impose on him a change of one parent for the other. Only in very unusual cases should the tie between him and his natural mother be broken.

A number of social workers maintain that even where there is physical violence in a home, their observations show that anxious authorities may be rash to step in and split the family up. The child's loss of bearings and identity can prove to be more serious than the occasional black eye. This is an extreme view, which is largely based on work in poorer areas and with under-privileged families. But the principle to which they point is not irrelevant elsewhere.

Sometimes a mother of a young child will explain her willingness to see him only at intervals along these lines: 'But Johnny had always seemed indifferent to me,' or 'We just don't seem to hit it off.' This is treating young children as if they were mature and could choose. Apparent lack of affection or indifference does not mean the child is not dependent.

Later on, a great deal can be said to depend on the emotional age of the child. He may be seven, but still feeling like a four-year-old. It also depends on brothers and sisters, and how close he is with them. Dividing up small brothers and sisters who have learnt to support, entertain and cherish each other during marital storms is a very bad risk. The other factors that should influence the decision are the likelihood of a settled home life after the proposed split; the degree to which close relations are available to help give continuity of affection and care; whether there are opportunities for contact with the 'lost' parent afterwards, and what problems this contact will pose. As the child gets older, other questions like education and close friends will enter into the discussions.

As the child matures, need for parents gradually merges into enjoying living with them, learning from them. It doesn't happen overnight, but gradually the child is strong enough to pick and choose when to make contact, rather than relying on regularity. He may prefer one parent to another, and at this stage 'hitting it off' with his parents is a valid concept. He may become anxious about other people's attitudes towards his mother, or father, or both. Then he will avoid bringing friends home, and radiate embarrassment at family parties. He may decide to shun his parents' company and spend as much time as he can with his friends. Sometimes he will boast about his independence. A precocious child may be doing all this at eight. Others may not show any of these feelings until puberty or beyond.

None of this means that one's child is mature enough to stand the shock of his parents separating and getting a divorce. These are mitigating circumstances rather than sufficient circumstances. Great care should be taken to cushion the child against the shock, even where he seems, superficially, to be better equipped than most to withstand it, and even where he positively welcomes the idea. The fact of the split may be harsher than he expects. Some guide-lines for helping children in these situations are given in the next chapter. Before that, some examples of what can happen to these children are worth considering, for the suggestions as well as for the warnings that they offer.

Philip

Philip was about eighteen months old when his parents' marriage started going seriously wrong. He was a perfectly normal, happy baby, as far as can be remembered. He was too young to notice, or be concerned by the fact that his mother came to the conclusion she had married the wrong man, while his father was getting increasingly fed up with what he regarded as gross neglect of their home.

Her attitude, in retrospect: 'It suddenly dawned on me that we had already gone through everything we had in common; and although he was quite happy for me to dedicate the rest of my life to cooking, mending and cleaning a house for a man, this was a horrifying outlook to me.' His attitude: 'While I was in love with her, I tried to persuade myself she wasn't a slut. But she could never keep a home—simply because she didn't want to.'

She walked out one Monday morning when Philip was asleep. She knew her mother-in-law would be arriving, so she left the door of the flat ajar, with a brief note of explanation propped against a milk bottle. According to the father, this included the phrase, 'Suggest you get Philip adopted, if you don't want all the nappies.' But she denies writing this.

For a while Philip was looked after by his grandmother and then he paid an extended visit to his father's cousin's family. When it became quite clear that Philip's mother had no intention of returning, arrangements were made for Philip to be fostered. All did not go smoothly at first, because the first foster parents suddenly realized, after having him for about five months, that they could not continue fostering (the husband lost his job and they had to move to a smaller home). Then followed a short spell at a children's home; and then a six-month period back with his father, who was living with a second woman on a kind of trial run, and judging whether this time there might be sufficient compatibility for a long-term, stable marriage. In fact, there wasn't. Shortly before his fourth birthday, then, Philip met the foster parents who have looked after him for the past three years.

When you first meet Philip he looks very much like a normal, healthy boy. He is good-looking, and wiry in a rather athletic way. In front of others, he stands awkwardly, and fidgets—but then so do many other seven-year-olds. He returns your greeting with silence, and a shy smile with his head turned at an angle from you. Clearly, he wants to get away.

Philip is not very good at talking, or at making friends. He reminds you rather of a stray cat who agrees to come in for a meal, but backs away desperately if you try to stroke him. He is polite, and nice to his foster parents, but not at ease, They say he has an uncanny way of making them feel nervous too.

It is the same at school apparently. His teacher feels that he is very unlikely to make much progress in her large class because he needs much more individual attention. She suspects he would benefit from remedial teaching, and negotiations are under way for getting him into a unit for disturbed children at an ESN school. The other children sense that he is in some way an outsider, because he won't give and take—in conversation, or activity—as they do. They call him 'stupid', despite his teacher's attempts to re-group the children in different sets round the room, and her encouragement to some of the more protective ones to draw him into their games and their projects. He has become resigned to being different, although occasionally he will lose his temper and lash out wildly at everybody. Recently, he has been further alienated from the others because he began slipping into the classroom during break and taking their things. It was never anything much—hair-slides, animal picture cards, a yoyo, a few small coins—but he was invariably discovered, and confronted by outraged classmates. Knowing something of his background, and being intelligent, his teacher was anxious to discourage him from doing it again without making him feel punished by the school and by society.

His foster parents have been trying very hard to do as much as possible with Philip. It is not easy, because he cannot learn things quickly, and loses patience. He enjoys television, but doesn't have much to say about the programmes he sees.

There is a lot of time to go yet, but it is obvious that Philip has had the kind of start to life that gives him many disadvantages. It is impossible to sort out exactly which influences or experiences have played which part in creating Philip's difficulties. He *may* have been less intelligent than others from birth; he *may* have suffered more from being shunted around from one house to another than he did by being separated from his mother. (From Philip's point of view, this is academic.) But he is a particularly unfortunate example of *mismanagement* of separation; and his development is by no means untypical of other children who have been separated from their mother, and in fact rejected, early in life. Most of his difficulties can be called consistent with a sense of loss of belonging, and a wariness about committing himself in the future to other people's friendship and affection.

A more promising example of a child surviving a broken home is Will.

Will

In Will's case, it was his father who left home—for the first time when he was one, and definitively when he was two. The circumstances were complex. Will's father antagonized his mother by experimenting with drugs, and being difficult to live with. He felt, on his side, that he was being bled of ambition to advance either academically or in a career by being encouraged to concentrate on tending his home in a London suburb. There was a series of confrontations and reconciliations, which became more and more dramatic. Eventually there was a court order restraining Will's father from 'molesting' his family any further.

67

Will's mother was helped by her parents, and her parents-in-law, in looking after Will. Although she needed to go to work, Will was always aware of her being close by, or coming back soon. She has not re-married.

Now, at six, Will sees his father about once a month. These reunions are even-tempered, and Will is very keen on them. He often plans when his father's next visit should be.

Will is good-looking, like Philip, but he gives the impression of being a clever child, who is very sensitive to atmosphere and changes of mood. He has developed some precocious social traits, such as changing the subject quickly and noisily if he senses that his father and mother are coming close to an argument.

At school he had a difficult first month or two. The other boys formed into groups more quickly than he did, so that he was a target for bullying. But Will worked through his problems, partly by using his tongue to make the others laugh, and be more interested in him, partly by learning to kick back when they kicked him. He is reasonably popular now, and enjoys school. His teacher regards him as bright.

He can be naughty, obstinate, querulous. His mother wonders whether it is because he lacks his father's presence that he has days when he seems to argue about everything he is asked to do, and not to do.

It is possible that Will is using this naughtiness to secure more attention from a mother who is leading a full life. He has, his father feels, learnt more ways than most children of flagging a grown-up's attention.

Will has developed some interesting fantasies about his father. Some of these he uses at school, and with his friends. His father has several cars, he tells them, all grander and more exotic than anything seen on the local roads. There is the same romantic touch in his comments about his friends. They are each described in terms that seem larger than life: they have no faults, they all do exciting things every week-end, and they are all—significantly—very loyal to him.

It is very difficult to see in Will very much more than a normal, rather clever child, who is averagely difficult at home, but perhaps a bit more sensitive and affectionate than most. The striking difference between him and Philip is that he is confident, where Philip has no confidence. This extends to anything which somebody needs to master if he is going to live a full life.

Many of those people who say that too much fuss is made of the problems of a child coming from a background of divorce or separation are genuinely thinking of their own circumstances, or of children like Will, who seems to be facing the future positively. But where the children appear to have come out of it well, there are usually some strong influences operating that have provided stability and compensation. Of course, human beings can rise superior to their troubles, *provided* they are given a decent chance to do so.

There are, on the other hand, people who claim that children of divorced parents are more likely to get divorced themselves. There is no clear-cut evidence on this, but there is evidence that a higher than average proportion of juvenile delinquents, and criminals, come from broken homes. Here again, to be fair, one should assume that it is the circumstances and aftermath of the break-up, rather than the simple fact of separation or divorce, that are to blame.

Six
Family Break-up
II: Some Advice

This is, of course, not a book on how to avoid separation. It would be a tempting one to try to write, but is best left to somebody better qualified. Anyone with young children, who feels the possibility of separation growing more threatening, needs advice of that kind. The National Marriage Guidance Council has highly skilled counsellors who undertake this service. This is a widespread organization, with over 130 'councils' across the United Kingdom. They do not promise to save marriages, or to make recommendations that the couple should definitely do this or that. Their skill lies in helping people to see more sides to their problems, so that they can get a better view of what their priorities are. Their advice extends to helping couples whose marriage has irretrievably broken down to arrange things for the best.

It is not a great deal of use telling people who are determined to leave each other how wrong they are. The same applies to a couple with a young child, who have reached the conclusion that one of them must go, and therefore the child must be separated from one or the other.

Social workers tend to put a lot of emphasis on keeping a child with his mother if at all possible. A lot of mothers, they point out, do a splendid job simply by being there. If they are sometimes rough with their children, at least the children learn what the danger signs are, and they often accept this as part of an imperfect, but stable, world. Magistrates sometimes view these social workers' recommendations with surprise. Why are they pleading for custody of children to remain vested in somebody who is of low intelligence; or poor; or insensitive; or with a criminal record; or in any other way apparently less than adequate to a comfortable, middle-class view? The answer is that they can judge, from their experience, the importance of preserving this bond during the early years.

Obviously there will be cases where the mother rejects the child, or has a personality problem of such a kind as to rule out her looking after him. But in normal circumstances advice has to start with the suggestion that she should keep custody.

Here is further advice, written as for a mother who is separating from her husband and keeping her child, or children. A lot of it applies to either parent, however.

a Even if she has to go out to work, she should try to be very close with her child: this means touching and cuddling him, reading to him, talking, singing or playing with him. This is written in full knowledge that she probably has very little spare time, and—after working hard during the day—deserves some well-earned rest. But in the effort to keep financially secure, and to keep up appearances, it is all too easy to lose touch with the main point of keeping the child: which is to make him feel happy in being her child.

b To help her do this, involving others in her family makes sense unless they are wholly incompatible with her or her child. This may mean swallowing some pride. It may mean overcoming shyness as well to ask a relation if she could possibly look after the child for a day or two in the week. But this can be important in two ways, if it works. First, it allows the mother more room to manoeuvre in planning the week for herself and her child as well as her work. Second, it means that there is a greater sense, for the child, of family in the background—even during the long day when the mother is out at work.

c Wherever she lives there is likely to be some provision made by the local authority for child-minding, if the child is below school age. This may take the form of a crèche, or a State nursery school (though these are few and far between), or a series of registered child-minders. The mother will usually have to go to them, rather than the other way round, although in the case of illness or difficulties in transport, the children's officer may be able to make special arrangements. It costs nothing to ask about these services. Later on— if, say, she suspects that the child-minder appointed is not doing a good job—it costs nothing to complain then, either. Just as it does not do to take the helpfulness of any individual official for granted, it makes no sense not to speak up when it is clear that something is inadequate or wrong.

(It is amazing how some mothers in this situation are shy about suggesting changes. In a nursery group in Kent, run by the local council for working mothers, a temporary staff replacement decided she disliked changing nappies. For a period of about two months, babies and toddlers would be handed back reeking in the late afternoon. The mothers looked at each other, and sighed. They were very polite, very British, and conscious of receiving a favour. But no one did anything, until a strong-willed newcomer to the group took a senior official in hand, led her from child to child one afternoon, and demanded, 'Can you sense that anything's wrong?' This did the trick.)

d There are a lot of economic pressures on a separated mother. She must find out about all possible sources of benefit from the State and claim them. The local office of the Department of Health and Social Security should be visited, to determine eligibility for Family Benefits and Family Income Supplement. The official there is paid to be a public servant, and this means respecting confidences on any personal details given. If there is difficulty about getting maintenance payments from the father, the Citizens' Advice Bureau will be able to advise. (Obviously, a solicitor can be asked to look into all these things, but that costs money.) A visit to the local Income Tax office is important, to ensure that all possible tax concessions are claimed.

e For a young child a sense of regular contact is very important. This doesn't mean that his mother should avoid anything that breaks up the rhythm: it means that the rhythm itself should *exist*. The child should know that, special circumstances apart, there are times in the day when his mother can be relied on to be there. When she cannot be there, there should, if possible, be someone looking after him whom he knows, in a place that he recognizes.

f The child will be working out his own compensations for lack of contact with his father. He may cultivate a particular friend—he may even *invent* a friend. Other similar behaviour includes new enthusiasms for, say, aeroplanes, that are suggestive of his father's maleness, if only at a fantasy level. A mother ought to try to share these interests, and listen to her child's more improbable outpourings sympathetically. Where appropriate, and where possible, she could mention to him some real things about his father and what he is doing, so that her child's imagination can feed on a better balance of reality and fantasy.

g Closely allied is this very basic advice: try not to paint an unpleasant picture of the father. Even when he is a scoundrel it does much more harm than good to make this clear to a child. Affinity with his father is always felt to some extent or other, even if the child dislikes him heartily. It is far better that he should have some positive points in his mind to feel later on that he might have inherited. It is also unfair to a child to draw him into an emotional frame of mind prematurely before he has developed some control over his emotions. When this happens he feels frustrated that nothing dramatic is done to right his mother's wrongs, and he is unable to adjust to his father's visits, because civilized behaviour is unintelligible.

It is often worth advising relations too not to be overcritical of the father. Grandmothers can be particularly tactless unless warned.

h Unless it is *proved* to be inadvisable, periodic contact with the child's father is very desirable. Knowing about the father directly is much healthier than compiling a mixture of vague memory and biased comment, and turning it into a strange picture to brood upon, over time. A child may ask for more contact with his father. Some compromise may be better than sticking rigidly to a court-imposed minimum: it is natural human behaviour to want to see somebody on impulse, and to increase the frequency when the two get on together. Following rigid rules (even if they happen to be convenient) is unnatural and suggests a strange sense of values.

i Many mothers are happy about an estranged father seeing their child every so often, provided that his new wife or friend does not make contact too. It is very natural to feel hostile towards her, and protective where the child is concerned. Contact with her seems like tacit approval of extra-marital activities, or second marriages. But is it not better for a child to satisfy his natural curiosity—which he will develop, whatever his mother's attitude—and meet the new wife or friend once or twice, than to ponder over a mystery woman, about whom questions are firmly discouraged?

j What, exactly, and how much should a child be told about the break-up of a marriage? Some things, for example violence, are best avoided in discussion, but most questions that a child puts deserve an honest answer. If his father has disappeared without explanation, it is pointless denying to a child that his whereabouts are unknown; that he is missed; that he might be coming back, or he might not. A very young child may not ask all these questions, and may, in fact, accept the disappearance as part of a scheme of things he does not seek to understand. Here it is usually unwise to provide information that the child does not actually ask for, if there is any chance that it will alarm him. Where possible, parents should agree on what to say. Certain key relatives should be briefed too, for consistency. Inevitably when the child is a good deal older he will want to know much, much more.

k It can help a young child greatly to keep the main items in his life constant after separation of his parents. Sometimes this is impossible, but where there is a choice, it is best to stick to the same house or flat as before; to keep the child sleeping in the same room—his own room; to arrange for him to keep seeing the same friends that he played with before. Remaining at the same school has a similar benefit in encouraging an optimistic view—that life is not completely disrupted. As a further step towards security and continuity, some parents decide to send their child to a boarding-school. This is a complex subject, covered in a separate chapter.

l A divorced woman has her own life to lead. Some quite clearly get 'possessed' by their children, and devote themselves exclusively to ensuring they are cared for fully. This can lead to producing a rather spoilt, possessive child, and to a big gap appearing in the woman's life when the child grows up. There is nothing inconsistent in giving one's child a great deal of affection and attention, and at the same time having one's own friends, and possibly marrying again.

There are no rules—except, perhaps, patience!—for getting a second partner to hit it off well with a child of the first marriage. The important things are that the new partner should want, genuinely, to become close to the child; and that there should be no despondency if this is not achieved immediately. Persistence pays.

m Finding oneself in the situation of having to provide and care for a child, or several children, alone, can bring depression as well as practical problems. It can sometimes make even the most maternal of women feel that somehow they have been cut off from a lot of life's richness and opportunity. At these times it is not difficult, although it seems unpleasant, to feel a certain resentment towards the child.

Feeling resentment is not the same as expressing it, which should be very carefully avoided. Some children living with one parent are under pressure to grow up quickly, to mature early so that the parent's burden is eased. This is one form that such resentment can take. It is dangerous, because it will colour his attitude towards his own marriage and his own children.

n A lot of people say, looking back at their own childhood,

that they could sense something was wrong long before separation and divorce actually occurred. This is part memory but part imagination. Those who have bitterest memories, however, are usually the children whose parents went through a lot of changes of mind, of temporary solutions, of a complex of hesitations, decisions, second thoughts, and third thoughts.

No one can blame a couple, with or without children, for trying new ways of reaching a better understanding. But young children should not be brought into the middle of the drama. They are unprepared for being told, one week, 'Everything's fine again, now—we're going back to live in our old house with Daddy', followed by (a month later), 'We cannot possibly live here any more.'

o Children of separated parents can be, and sometimes are, fostered or taken into care, which may mean spending a long time in a residential home. However good some homes may be this is an enormous risk to them. Cutting off a child's ties with both his parents is a very desperate step.

Parents' separation is, of course, undesirable for a child, unless the alternative is obviously going to be worse, but there is a lot of evidence to suggest that how a separation is organized may be almost as important, in the long-term effects on a child, as the separation itself.

One case history is appended to show just how unpleasant the consequences of a badly botched separation can be. It scarcely needs a commentary: most of the points in the preceding pages are highlighted by it.

Nicola

Nicola was four when her mother first made her put on her coat saying, 'Come on, we're moving down the road.' She remembers a strange scene in which her father stood outside a nearby house, shouting up to the window at which she watched with her mother. It was bizarre, and it stuck in her mind although at the time it meant very little.

She had been taught to fear, distrust and hate her father, even before this episode occurred. She can recall his trying to be nice to her, and coaxing her into the car to go for a drive. This ended with her pounding on the windows, screaming to be released. Much later, all her questions about him elicited comments such as, 'You can never believe a word he says,' and 'He's the reason why we are so poor.' When at sixteen she tracked him down, impelled by curiosity, and said she was visiting him, her mother suggested, 'Ask him for some money. He owes us a lot.'

The separation when Nicola was four lasted only a week. There was another, then there was a period of indecision, and then a final break which meant they moved in with Gran. This was where Nicola lived for over eleven years. The house was occupied by four generations of women, including Gran's mother. Each grew to dislike each of the others. Her mother used to disappear for intervals and there would be sharp recriminations on her return.

Much of her mother's frustration and resentment was taken out on Nicola. Knowing her daughter was much attracted to a kitten, relying on it for company, she once seized it by the scruff and marched into the lavatory, shouting, 'I'm fed up with this. I'm going to drown it.' She pulled the chain. It was only a bad joke, but since Nicola was just eight at the time it gave her nightmares for weeks.

Gran arranged for Nicola to receive some psychiatric help once a week at a hospital. This went on, with a number of breaks, between the ages of seven and eleven. She was encouraged by a series of doctors to be less nervous, less frightened of the world, more confident about school, which had thoroughly alarmed her.

'Your father never wanted you', was part of her indoctrination, when her puberty was explained. This, she was given to believe, was a major cause of the breakdown of her mother's marriage. The implication was reinforced by her stepfather's dislike of her.

Nicola continues her story in these terms. 'I got married myself as soon as I could. To get away. I was no good at anything, so it had to be marriage, I suppose. It meant I could be free from that terrible house. I didn't know what I was doing. I married at twenty-three, and I absolutely devastated this poor bloke.

'It was terrible. I suppose I inherited it. I had to produce the same kind of hell for him that my mother had inflicted on my father. I told him he was mean about money, unambitious, lazy, the kind of man who sinks without trace. I'm really sorry for him now. Anyway, we finished it all in two years, and I suddenly found myself divorced.'

About this time she went back to see her father again, after a long interval. It was only then that she managed to break through the embarrassment that had made conversation so difficult before.

'It dawned on me that he was really nice. My mind had been poisoned against him. We got on well for about a year—before he died.'

Nicola had the courage to refuse to rejoin her mother after her divorce. She moved in with another divorcee, who has three children and is managing to bring them up by herself. This is a cheerful house, where Nicola was genuinely surprised at the way this family could relax, and laugh with each other. This made her feel distinctly more optimistic about life.

Now Nicola has an interesting job, and shares a flat with another young woman. She feels more secure about being independent, and makes friends more easily. Relations with her mother are bad, but most of the debris of the past is beginning to disappear.

This is in spite of suffering from a kind of separation in which most of the rules in the book were broken, one after another. Some parents, like Nicola's father, find themselves unable to intervene, while they suspect their children are being badly brought up by their estranged partner. Anticipating this situation is far easier than doing anything about it later.

It would be very wrong to suggest that Nicola is typical. Many more children are considerately treated, and the effects of family break-up are far less cruel to them. The problems in her family, however, were typical enough. The encouraging part of Nicola's story is her determination, and success at re-creating her life the hard way.

Seven
Fostering and Adoption

Sometimes it is clear to a mother that she cannot, for one reason or another, provide an adequate home for her baby or child. Sometimes the parents take this view jointly. In these cases the mother has to decide whether she wants to have her child adopted or fostered.

If a child is adopted, this is, except in very rare circumstances, forever. The mother has to realize that the child will never be hers again. There are many safeguards, some of which the law insists on, to check that the adoptive parents will be suitable, and that the child will be properly looked after in their home. Until these safeguards have been properly applied, and the court order is made, adoption can be stopped. But once the process is complete it is immutable.

A mother who wants the child to remain hers, and to be able to look after him again some time, will need to think in terms of fostering. Of its nature, this is a temporary arrangement. Every so often, changes in the law are discussed which would give long-term foster parents adoption rights in certain circumstances, but this is not at present the case. The natural mother can almost always reclaim him, unless it can be shown that this would be detrimental to the welfare of the child, whatever the court proceedings instituted by foster parents or a local authority.

Adoption *has* to be official: without a court order, it cannot happen. But fostering can be official or unofficial.

Normally these courses are thought of in connection with the children born of unmarried mothers, but there is a wide range of situations which can lead to them—from desertion, or poverty, to the mother's death. The largest single group of cases where a child is 'received into care' (a pre-condition for adoption, placement in a community home, and for most fostering arrangements), is that of young children whose mother has a short-term illness (one in three) or a confinement (one in nine). This kind of arrangement is usually temporary, however, and this chapter will concentrate more on situations which could lead to permanent separation.

Either action is obviously a serious interruption in the relationship between a mother and child. For a mother to decide on either, she will need to be in very considerable difficulties, or else a rather unusual person. She will be anxious to know how likely it is that her child will be able to develop normally, and lead a happy life.

With adoption, the first point is that a mother who gives up her baby into care cannot be absolutely certain that he will be adopted. For several reasons, among which is the greater knowledge and availability of contraception, fewer babies are now available for adoption, and there is a long waiting-list of would-be adoptive parents with many adoption societies and local authorities. But this is no guarantee that a particular baby will not be brought up in a children's home. There is still difficulty in placing coloured children, and those with physical handicaps or delicate health. Anyone with a suspected mental handicap, however slight, may have very little chance indeed of being adopted. Within these categories, girls are adopted sooner than boys, and younger children rather than older.

It is not the end of the world to be brought up in a children's home, but there is no question that a normal family upbringing is to be preferred. In the more institutional and impersonal homes there is always the danger of 'Long-Stay Personality' [1] setting in. Where this is supplemented with fostering of some kind it must be to the child's advantage. One encouraging trend is towards fostering a child from a home during, say, the school holidays. This puts the child—when the arrangement works, and the child and his foster family get used to each other—almost in the position of going to boarding-school. It offers the chance

[1] See Chapter 4.

of avoiding what often afflicts children in care when they grow up—an idealized and unrealistic view of family life, and expectations that lead to disillusion when marrying and setting up home.

Assuming that the child is adopted as a baby, it is very unlikely that the mother will have more than a fleeting glimpse of the adoptive parents. She will, however, be told a good deal about them by the local children's officer, or by the Adoption Society by whom the baby is placed. They will reassure her about the kind of people they are, and about their home. But she will have to take this on trust.

What safeguards has she got that her baby will be loved and cared for?

The main point is that adoptive parents are thoroughly screened beforehand. The prospective father and mother are interviewed both separately and together. They fill in forms about themselves; they get their doctor to fill in a searching questionnaire about their health; they receive visits from the council or the society concerned; and if they have children already, these are seen and talked to as well. It is rare for applicants to receive a baby with a view to adoption before they have waited a considerable time. This is sometimes explained to them as due to waiting-list problems: while this may be true, it is customary to make sure that the applicants are still eager to adopt six months after they first applied. Any wavering in enthusiasm is obviously a bad sign.

When a child is placed in the applicants' home, there is a minimum of three months' wait between application for a court order and the granting of the order which would make the adoption permanent. During this period visits are made to note how the child is settling in and the atmosphere in the home.

One of the documents that has to be laid before the court is a form signed by the child's natural mother, and/or father, according to circumstances, indicating that consent has been given. Without this consent, which has sometimes been withdrawn at the last moment, the adoption cannot go through. If the parents have disappeared, however, their consent can be overlooked provided that the court can be satisfied that serious efforts have been made, including advertising, to locate them. Consent cannot be given by the mother within three months after the birth, since it is recognized that women are particularly liable after childbirth to serious emotional problems which affect judgment.

A great deal of care, in fact, goes into ensuring that a mother really wants to give up her child, and that the home which the child joins is a welcoming one.

The same applies to the screening of foster parents, particularly where young children are concerned. But this only goes for foster parents who are given children to look after by local authorities, and by large children's homes and societies. Anyone who makes a private arrangement with another family to look after their child can only go by their own impressions.

It is very difficult, even knowing about these safeguards, for a mother to predict whether she will ultimately regret giving up her baby. She is bound to have some advisers telling her to do one thing, and possibly others who urge her to do differently. If she surrenders her child within the first six weeks behaviour problems are more likely to be avoided, and the mother does not get time to develop a routine of looking after her baby. Not being in the habit of enjoying him she does not feel the parting as keenly as she might. But there is a sense of loss, which is unpredictable, depending as it does both on personality and on the mother's later life.

There is remarkably little research work conducted into the development of adopted children—less, for example, than there is on children brought up in care. The vast number of factors that can affect children as they grow up makes it very difficult to assess the influence of adoption as such. In most cases it is quite clear that the influence of adoption comes into play only with older children, since a very young baby is not old enough to register the changeover in such a way as to build up complex reactions to it. With children adopted later the picture is not so clear-cut. In their situation, moreover, adoptive parents differ in the way they introduce and talk about the fact of adoption, the children vary in what they demand to know, and other children in the family vary in the use they make of this information.

Some problems that adopted children share can be called modal: i.e. they recur time and again in case histories with minor variations. They are clearly illustrated by Mark, although it should be stressed that they do not usually take such an extreme form.

Mark

At the age of two, Mark was placed with an adoption society by a woman who found herself alone and in considerable difficulties —in terms of money, health and a place to live. He was lucky in that he had immediate appeal, being blond, chubby, with large green eyes and a soulful look, according to photographs. A middle-aged couple, who had one son aged four, and wanted another but could not manage it, adopted him very quickly.

They knew it was riskier to adopt a toddler than a baby, but they felt equal to the challenge. Moreover they argued that Mark would be a better companion for their first son, Terry, if he were close in age.

Looking back on Mark as a little boy, the adoptive parents remember that he was very affectionate, eager to be cuddled, and worked hard at getting attention. He had a wide range of facial expressions, and he quickly learned how to make his parents laugh. Certain situations would make him particularly anxious—such as the suggestion that a mealtime was late or might be missed. By and large, however, he seemed contented, and not a nervous child.

Mark remembers his parents in his early childhood as being very kind, and very concerned to make him happy. 'I was probably spoilt, by comparison with Terry', is his verdict.

He remembers the sudden realization—when he was four or five—that if he took something from his elder brother and his parents were in the room, Terry was virtually powerless to get it back. He remembers the scene which led up to this—Terry trying to retrieve a toy gun, and his parents stopping Terry from taking it, as soon as he, Mark, started to cry. He flushed with pleasure at his new-found power, and at the same time felt guilty about the expression of disgust on Terry's face.

Very early on his mother told Mark that he was adopted. He thinks he was about three at the time. He wanted to know who his real mother was. Here, however, his adoptive parents could give him no information. He thought a lot about it, and made up stories. There had to be a secret, he decided, which explained why his adoptive parents would say nothing, and seemed to resent his persistent questioning.

Mark showed he was more intelligent than Terry in various ways, and they preferred different games. When Mark went to school, he proved to have great academic determination. 'My teacher once found me' (at eight) 'staying in the classroom after school, and changing each of the sums I'd done wrong, so that it looked as if I'd got all the answers right, and changing the crosses to ticks. I blushed like mad, but the teacher only said, "Why are you doing that, Mark? You're very good at sums—you don't really need to."'

Mark and Terry developed different interests and different friends. When Terry suffered the indignity of seeing his younger brother joining his class, he was outraged. Terry became unhappy, unless he was playing football with his particular pals.

Terry failed his 11-plus exam, went to a secondary modern school, scraped one O-level in English Language, and left school at fifteen. He became an apprentice at a printer's, and developed a fair talent for getting the best out of printing machinery. He has a supervisor's job, enjoys it, and is popular with the others at the works. He married young, has two small children, but feels no ambition to land a more responsible job, or to get much more money. He is happy, and gets on well with his parents. In the past five years, he has seen Mark only twice.

Mark had some difficulty about studying at home, especially when he was close to his A-levels. But he got three of these in languages, and went to a university in the North. On graduating with second-class honours he found he had even less in common with his parents than he had suspected. They were proud of him but considered that 'his head was turned' by success. He married a girl he met at college, who came from an upper middle-class family. The wedding met with disapproval all round. It did not last long, either, for which Mark tends to blame himself.

'I was much too young, and stupid about it,' says Mark. 'I was very much in love, and I believed everything would be wonderful. I took her assurance that she wouldn't mind coming down in the world, and living in a small flat, at face value. Then I believed that she would be happy with the baby all day long, while I worked all day, with a post-grad course in the evening. We wanted a kind of intellectual salon, and only succeeded in embarrassing anyone who visited us with our rows.'

Mark is successful: he is on the board of a thriving company and is widely respected in the profession he took up. He is also discontened: divorced, rootless and anxious about how to fill his week-ends.

It is interesting to speculate how Mark would have developed had he been brought up by his natural parents. He might have been living with people who understood his intellectual interests better; this is on the assumption that there was an hereditary factor involved. An alternative view is that it was by reason of his knowing that he was adopted, and passed on, and rejected, that he developed his determination to show his cleverness, to win prizes and come out top. There is something to be said for both views. The fact of hereditary intelligence is not nowadays disputed: many who are involved in adoption certainly believe in it. However, the *extent* to which genes programme intelligence is open to argument. Determination to succeed is a character trait that is often observed by psychiatrists among those who feel they have to compensate for something important. 'Need achievement' in Mark is certainly high. Had he been brought up in a home, as opposed to being adopted statistics are against the possibility that he would have taken A-levels, much less gone to university.

Part of his 'need achievement' meant establishing an idealistic household—he wanted a beautiful, intelligent wife, with whom he would live forever in perfect harmony, while pursuing both a business and an academic career, and moving rapidly up the socio-economic scale. Determination stops winning as soon as other people are closely involved. Inability to see people realistically lay at the root of Mark's marital troubles. Right now, he seems capable of succeeding at anything except deep personal relationships.

Another side to Mark is his eagerness to please. Many adopted children at school are noted by teachers as being very disarming in their ways. They have often developed a precocious charm. This is interpreted as making efforts to ensure that they are 'in', accepted and—ultimately—loved, because they have awareness, however vague, that at a critical point they were not accepted but rejected.

Developing ways of pleasing people on a short-term basis need not exclude preparation for making lasting relationships, but if it becomes an obsession it can squeeze out sensitivity to other people's feelings and wishes, which is what makes a close partnership possible. This is not inevitable with adopted children, by any means. But it is common enough to have been noted.

It is not the end of the world to be like Mark. Some would argue that industry, or society, requires some Marks, with their high need achievement, to supply a dynamic to life. But Terry's small house seems much happier than Mark's large flat. And the people in Terry's life seem happier too.

By and large, a couple who want to adopt a child are very anxious to make a success of it. If this were not the case, why would they go to the trouble of having interviews, getting onto a waiting list, demanding to know why they are being kept waiting, and so forth? Their eagerness is, in one sense, the best guarantee that a mother can have, when she is giving up her child, learns that he is definitely to be adopted, and is asked to sign a paper giving her consent.

It is a matter of luck, however, whether the adoptive parents will be really well matched to her child in intelligence terms and whether they will be sensitive and sensible about telling her child about his adoption. Mark's parents got the first part of this right: they made it clear to him at an early age that he was adopted. (Leaving it to puberty, or later, runs the risk of making it seem a great shock.) But after arousing his curiosity they became embarrassed, and discouraged further questions, which helped make it all a great mystery for him, and contributed to his sense of not belonging with them. In other adoptive families, adopted children have been helped to come to terms with their background, just as if it were being tall, or having red hair.

Similarly, while there have been many cases of adoptive parents being perplexed or disappointed because of their adopted child's talents and interests being very unlike those of their other children, or their own, others will watch with delight to see what unexpected things their adopted child will contribute. Adoption societies encourage this attitude. They are usually very careful to point out to prospective adopters that the child may fall short of what they would like in terms of academic brightness. If this is the case, it is better to have started out with an open mind, and to know that you might need to encourage practical or athletic achievement rather than a love of books.

When a young unmarried mother feels pressure on her to have her baby adopted, one argument that recurs is that her child may never experience a father in her home. As only *couples* are allowed to adopt, adoption guarantees at least a father.

There is little doubt that a father is desirable: just how *necessary* he is to a child's development will depend on several things. A father complements the home, and shows by his presence and example, together with the mother, how a family knits together. This is a simple, long-drawn-out lesson that has a profound influence. Depending on the father, this can be for bad, as well as for good. A boy will also identify with his father—to *some* extent, even when he seems to reject his father. A girl will normally get the first reactions to her femininity from her father. Without him both will inevitably lose a sounding-board, from which to judge how their actions are treated by authority. The importance of this loss depends primarily on the mother, who can compensate them for it in various ways; on their close friends in the community; on their kind of school, where contact may be anything from close to impersonal; and so forth. The child's personality too is an obvious factor, as is the presence of an older brother.

If a mother is fulfilling part of a second role as well as her own, her time has to be tightly channelled. She may have to show interest, for example, in football, when she would prefer some time on her own. This kind of demand is inevitable, and it is as well to try to foresee it when approaching the decision of whether to keep a baby or not.

In these circumstances, it helps a great deal to talk to mothers who decided to keep their children. They ought to know what it is going to be like.

Douglas and his mother

'I decided, just as I was going into hospital, that I wasn't going to give up my baby. For some reason I was convinced he was going to be a boy. Suddenly I knew, *knew* that he was mine, and going to stay mine. My mother smiled indulgently, because it had all been arranged with an adoption society beforehand, and she thought I would soon snap out of it.

'The testing time was in the maternity ward. Everybody else was getting visits from their husbands, except me and one other mum. I tried talking to her, but she was terribly nervous.

'My mother came in one day with somebody from the council Children's Office who she knew personally. This was her way of persuading me that whatever my feelings about it, the best thing was to give up Douglas. They were going to tell me about this couple who'd been waiting and waiting for five years, unable to have any children. I just told them I wasn't having any, and I remember the nurse coming over because she thought I was too upset, or upsetting her ward or something.

'Anyway, I had a very good friend from where I work. She asked around and found a lady with a grown-up son and a spare room. I moved in there as soon as I could. They were terribly kind. . . .

'I was completely in the dark about family allowances and income tax and all that kind of thing. Nobody tells you anything, you've got to find out. But this lady—she'd had to do most of it for herself after her husband died. She went down to the tax office with me, and all that.

'. . . The worst thing, I suppose, was feeling tied down. If I wanted to go to a party or a dance or anything like that, I had to work out every minute of it. It was all right when Doug was a baby, and I was with Mrs L.' (see above) 'but when he was older and I had to collect him from the nursery, bring him back, cook something, get a tray for the baby-sitter, have a bath with Doug, almost, put him to bed, eat something, do my hair, put on a nice dress—and then find Doug was ill, so I had to cancel everything, and go out some other night. . . .'

Doug was a very popular boy, but there were problems over discipline, which grew particularly bad when he was five. Once he started school he seemed to adopt a double standard: in class he was angelic, at home he was rude and disobedient. His mother sensed that he was all right for most of the time that she did things with him, but paid her back whenever she turned to her own interests, or simply to talk to somebody on the telephone.

This was complicated by her becoming increasingly friendly with a man who eventually proposed to her and married her. Children in Doug's position, particularly only children who are boys, can become very hostile to a possible rival for their mother's love. As soon as Doug realized this man was a permanent guest, and would soon be his stepfather, he became much more pleasant to live with. This was partly because he liked and respected this man, but partly because it meant an end to indecision.

The improvement in Doug's behaviour dated from establishing a happy relationship with his stepfather. But sometimes, even without this factor, fatherless children who have seemed 'impossible' for a long time suddenly become much more reasonable. What seems to happen is that they take longer than other children to adapt to the principle that they cannot rely on constant attention, and that as they get older the periods of non-attention must lengthen. They fight for more contact with their mother, and court punishment, even, in order to get it. Then, when they are more mature in their understanding of their mother's situation there is sometimes a sudden change—almost as if a kind of compromise has been worked out. Outside interests play a part in this. Early on, they are aware of other children doing things that they are prevented from doing—e.g. being driven to the seaside by Daddy. This is in itself frustrating. As they get older, they compensate by getting more chance to play, to do things, in the neighbourhood and at school, because they can be left longer, and can adapt to more situations. But undoubtedly the major factor in this is how far the mother's enthusiasm for keeping her child has continued. If she becomes bitter about her lost chances, even if she does not outwardly treat him as an albatross, he will sense this. His defence, then, will be what is called 'bad behaviour'

Doug's mother takes a lot of pride in her son. 'If I called him the best thing that's happened to me, it wouldn't be fair on my husband, would it?' she says. 'Or on our little girl. But despite everything, even though it meant a big bust-up with my parents, I don't think I ever made a better decision than to keep him.'

She was luckier than some. She had good friends of her own age, who helped her get a home started. Her firm took her back after she had had Douglas, and let her get work finished in the lunch hour and at home, so that she could take her son to the council nursery and collect him at the right time. But if she had not been so determined, none of these advantages would have appeared, and they would not in themselves spell out success. On the debit side, she had no help or encouragement from her parents—but she overcame this.

She was able to get married too. This is less easy for a woman with a child. There is an argument that a man who takes on such a responsibility may be more mature and a worthier partner. But there is an obvious danger in the woman feeling that she is receiving a kind of favour when offered marriage: this is an unsound basis for any partnership. Then, if she feels desperate about marriage, she may be tempted to consider somebody who takes against her child. This might mean a disastrous union for all three parties.

These issues cannot be foreseen, particularly by a pregnant, unmarried woman who has many other thoughts on her mind concerning the present, rather than the future. But they are worth considering nonetheless even if only because this helps someone understand her own nature, and her priorities in life.

The National Council for the Unmarried Mother and her Child exists to help single mothers, and their children, in practical ways. Local authority social workers are beginning to have greater involvement with unmarried pregnant women—before the event, when practical planning is needed. The National Council are always open to consultation, and will try to help sort out the possibilities of getting suitable accommodation.

The first point is that many women, whose maternal desire is very strong, have brought up, and always will bring up, their own children in the most unfavourable circumstances. Their children will be their main reward. Society has more respect for them nowadays, although relatives, neighbours and the community at large are still capable of callous attitudes towards them. To be successful takes determination; being prepared to negotiate working hours with employers, and nursery or baby-minding facilities with local councils; a practical sense when finding somewhere to live, and making it into a happy home with more love than money or time. Help from grandparents is welcome when it comes, but is short-term. There are many cases where the baby sees more of the grandmother as he grows up, because his mother is out at work. Unconsciously, a really maternal grand-mother will 'take over': this can bring tensions, divided loyalties, spoiling . . . unless mother and grandmother can be very objective about their feelings.

If the mother lacks this determination, that is basically the answer to the dilemma. There are plenty of determined couples around who badly want to adopt. They, in turn, will have a better chance of success if the mother makes her decision quickly, and sticks to it. This is not a plea for people to refuse to acknowledge their mistakes, when they feel sure they have made them. Rather, it is a plea to work out a point of view about one's life, con-sidering both the practical and the emotional side, and then to live that life.

At this moment, the proportion of illegitimate births where the mother is below sixteen is increasing steadily. This is partly a by-product of younger maturation. There are thirteen-year-old, even twelve-year-old, mothers in the United Kingdom now.

Abortion is put forward as a solution to this, but the long-term mental effects of having an abortion, when at this age, are largely unknown. One can guess that they must be considerable. The same can be said for child-birth, although that has the advantage of being natural, and an achievement. This is outside the scope of this book, but the issue has to be raised, because the basic question of whether or not to take a baby from a young teenager, and in what circumstances, must be increasingly urgent over the next five years, if trends in statistics are anything to go by.

When a mother has taken on the responsibility of bringing up her child circumstances may change in such a way as to make it difficult to carry on. She may be deserted by her husband, or become ill, or poor. This is one of the main situations where fostering comes in.

Short-term fostering presents relatively few problems. There is some agreement over time. The older a child is, the more he will understand the arrangement. A young child may be resentful and tearful at first, but the chances are that it will seem far better than going into hospital, what with lots of individual attention, and an identifiable mother-substitute. Careful preparation, for him to get used to the house, and to his foster-mother, obviously helps.

Long-term fostering may be, and usually is, 'open-ended'. The mother, parent or guardian has the right to withdraw the child at any time, unless a court decides that the circumstances are such that he needs to be kept 'in care'. To be a long-term foster parent requires a rare degree of philosophic detachment. However much one might claim at the outset, 'I know the score. Johnny will be with us for a few years, maybe, and then—suddenly—he'll be taken away when his mother gets better. We must expect that'— it is a different matter when that moment suddenly comes. Talking to foster parents who loved, and needed, a particular child in their family, is like talking to people who have been involved in a major accident, and have been bereaved.

Millie

Mr and Mrs Wool were unable to have children. Because Mr

Wool had had TB in his teens, and despite his making an apparently full recovery, they were advised that they would not be accepted as adoptive parents. But this did not deter them from fostering. Curiously, they were introduced to a two-year-old little girl, Millie, who was in delicate health herself. She was one of six children, in an Anglo-Indian family, who lived in a three-room flat. The Health Visitor put it to Millie's parents that they should consider having Millie fostered, and they agreed.

By all accounts, Millie was a very lively and lovable child. On arrival at the Wools' house, she seemed very frail and nervous. But within half an hour, she was running round their sitting-room, laughing, looking at everything, and asking questions in an accent that was difficult to understand. Because the Wools had to rack their brains to understand her, she barely stopped for an answer, but sped off to the next delight.

She exhausted herself very quickly, and Mrs Wool had to watch carefully for signs that she was losing breath. When this happened, Millie had to be picked up, quietened down, and put gently but firmly to bed.

Gradually, Millie got stronger, and as she did so the language problem eased. The Wools marvelled at her ability to pick up adult phrases and use them accurately. She burst into their con-versations in the evening, determined to be an active part of the family, every hour of the day.

She never said much about her parents or her family although she admitted to missing them, sometimes. She was very com-posed during her mother's visits, which were about every six weeks. When her favourite sister came too, however, she was particularly pleased.

There were two children of her age a few doors away, with whom she got on very well.

It seemed amazing to the Wools that there were very few behaviour problems. 'Looking back, it's almost as if she'd known we had to enjoy all the time we had together, while it lasted.'

When Millie was nearly five, Mrs Wool contacted the Child Guidance Centre to ask their advice on primary schools. (There was a local State school, and a private school, with smaller classes,

93

both nearby: which would be better for Millie, given her health difficulty?) A week later, she was told by the Centre to expect Millie's parents to call within the next two days, to take her away. The Centre was sorry, but of course they could do nothing: they understood that Millie was being sent to Glasgow, to be looked after by an aunt.

The Wools were utterly stunned, because they had never foreseen that this could happen so suddenly, or that they would be so shocked by it. A week after Millie's departure (at which Millie herself had broken down), Mr Wool contacted the Child Guidance Centre again. Could he possibly have Millie's aunt's address in Glasgow? Millie had been particularly fond of a budgerigar, and he wanted to drive up to take it to her. The Centre said they would try to help. Two days after that, Mr Wool was telephoned by the Centre, to be informed that Millie had died.

In addition to their loss, the Wools were left with this mystery to ponder. Was it the long coach trip; the bitter March weather; insensitive treatment; heartbreak; or had something been going wrong with her chest, which they had not spotted at home? They have spent the last few years weighing up these possible factors, and having daydreams in which Millie's death turned out to be a fabrication invented by parents who were jealous of their influence. They now keep a dog.

*   *   *

Long-term foster parents are perhaps society's biggest gamblers. When they begin, they may not know how high the stakes are going to be. They (or the local authority) can apply through the courts to keep their child. An important case was taken as high as the House of Lords in 1971: here judgment was given in favour of the foster parents, on the grounds that moving the child (then seven) to a foreign country would be too disturbing in the circumstances. But legislators are caught on the dilemma of not wanting to limit natural parents' rights.

Going from one home to another is scarcely likely to improve a child's security. A feeling of rejection is possible, sometimes compounded with a feeling of failure or guilt. Foster parents with a lot of experience tend to agree that these children worry about their status: and when they understand that they are competing on level terms with other children in the family they become relieved, happier and more manageable.

Research suggests that disturbed children; children over four; those whose mothers recently died; and those who have a history of moving from house to house, are less likely to do well when fostered. If they are the youngest child in a foster home, that helps. Curiously, foster parents who are lower down the socio-economic scale seem to have more success at fostering. But the system is largely successful, and important for a society that cares about the homeless and the under-privileged.

Eight
Boarding-schools

A boarding-school is a typically British institution. Other countries have boarding-schools but many were copies of what were developed in the United Kingdom, and most people in most other countries avoid sending children to boarding-schools while they are still young. For the vast majority, boarding starts with going to college, but in the United Kingdom there are about 150,000 children at boarding-schools, and about 10 per cent of these are aged under ten while some start at five.

Like many other long-standing institutions which still have a claim on public attention today, boarding-schools have strong devotees and strong detractors. A large part of the arguments about them has to do with the divisions they help to create in society—i.e., they are criticized for fostering class-consciousness, both among those who go to them, and among those who realize they were excluded from them. This is mostly outside the terms of reference for this book but not completely. The other main points of dispute are about the effects that an enclosed society has on personality development, and whether there is unnecessary unhappiness, and later behaviour and personality problems resulting from entering it very young.

In the past there was less debate about whether boarding was a good or a bad thing in itself. Those who suffered at the hands of bullies, perverts, indifferent staff, and the tedium of highly organized but dull week-ends, tended to blame the particular school (or the particular house within the school) rather than the system itself. Blaming the system would have hit at oneself for not being a strong enough character to appreciate it. The majority of the upper middle class genuinely saw the boarding-school as an important element in training, both for encouraging preservation of British tradition, and for keeping the élitist class élite.

Attacks on boarding-schools as such came from those with a strong social conscience (e.g. George Orwell), which made the issue one of left versus right, rather than consideration of what is the best way to bring up children. An exception was E. M. Forster, who observed over fifty years ago that whereas boys generally left public boarding-schools with sound physique, and with a fair education, they emerged with 'undeveloped hearts'. This has become an area of increasing concern—that boys (and to a lesser extent girls) who are educated in close communities where emotion is frowned on, and where individuality is discouraged in favour of group activities, lose a sense of what is natural to express to other people, and react to each other superficially. Some, of course, have hotly denied this charge. Others have been anxious to develop schools where this danger is avoided, and 'progressive' schools have to a large extent been organized so that boarders should not lack for 'heart'.

Girls' boarding-schools are a comparatively late development. Many have gained from having no traditions to defend; they could introduce measures to protect the individual care of their pupils—and, ultimately, their individuality—according to advice from contemporary educationalists and psychologists, without being labelled 'cissies' or 'cranks'.

When people discuss boys who have been to public boarding-schools, conversation often breaks down because each has a separate idea of what a typical product is like. The schools themselves vary enormously, from strict, authoritarian establishments to democratic experimental units with a minimum of regulations. The boys, too, obviously differ enormously.

There are, however, some common elements among one segment of ex-boarders, who are not by any means typical of the total output, but who are similar enough to each other to be worth mentioning. This group is one which is thought to gain most from boarding-school. They have a history of separation from one parent, or both parents, and are entered into boarding-school particularly early. It is perfectly possible to argue that separation experiences as much as boarding-school contributed towards their distinct personality. In each case, there are obviously many factors at work—but there are plenty of cases where the most significant factor seems to be premature entry into a rigid institution. Here is an example:

Bob

Bob was very attached to his father, who died when he was four. His mother did not re-marry. She was anxious that her son should not be without male influence in his upbringing. This, together with a feeling that a public boarding-school would give him a solid, dependable world to grow up in, led her to enter him as a boarder at R school, at the age of seven.

Bob's sister remembers him as a great friend, when she was very young. An aunt's observations also suggest that, although he was shocked and unhappy for a few months after his father's death, he was a reasonably well-adjusted and happy little boy by the time he was five and six. He was open, friendly, and expressed himself cheerfully and well.

At R, Bob was singled out by some older boys as a good target for a few laughs. He had arrived with a teddy bear, to which he was very attached. Within a week he was begging the matron to hide it away because he had been teased mercilessly about it. But he could not hide his blond hair. This inspired the nickname 'pretty girl', with which he was chased around the grounds of R.

In his house there was a system within the system. The bigger boys expected instant obedience, the choicest items of tuck, from the weaker ones' tuck-boxes, and help with any house chores they were given. They reinforced their rule by dragging reluctant ones into what they called a 'torture-chamber', a disused coal-hole, without hindrance from the housemaster, who believed in letting boys fight their own battles. Provided the ethos of stiff upper lip was preserved, at the superficial level, he was content.

Bob's character underwent a fairly rapid change in certain respects. He learned to be retiring and unobtrusive. He kept his

feelings to himself, because he had discovered the dire retribution
meted out to anyone who sneaked to matron. When his aunt saw
him during the first holidays he seemed 'mouselike'. He was
more tidy, and more correct in his ways.

There were longer-term effects too. These included a loss of
contact with his younger sister. She asked him a lot about R, but
he dismissed her attentions more and more summarily, until
reaching the point of declaring 'You wouldn't understand it.
You're just a girl'.

This was not matched with any striking gains in friendships at
R. He only talked about his classmates under pressure. Even when
they made him laugh they meant little to him.

He learned to survive, to make defensive alliances, to put up a
fight, to enjoy sport, and to boss the juniors when it was his turn
to do so. 'It makes me seem rather vindictive, I suppose,' he will
disclose now. 'But I remember thinking, as Cranley and I held a
junior down and Gray larruped him for being cheeky to us, that
it was only fair, after what I'd been put through.'

Bob is now nearing forty. He is a bachelor, working in a large
insurance company. When he left school he joined the Navy. This
delighted him for five years, but then the life palled. He wanted
to get married, and have a more settled existence in England.
The insurance company offered him very little money to join
their ranks—'but it seemed a good set-up. I mean, you've got to
respect that sort of place'.

Twice he has been engaged to be married but twice it was
broken off. His sister has tried to get close to him on occasion
but he blushes, turns white and stammers whenever he is pushed
to talk about his personal emotions. On her advice he has sought
psychiatric help once, but 'felt silly', and called it off.

A lot of the time he seems happy, and content with life. That is
when he is meeting his acquaintances in a bar at the golf club, or
at a local political group. He has many acquaintances, but no
friends, so far as can be told. He refutes his sister's claim that he is
lonely: his diary, he points out, is packed with detail. Indeed, it
is. But it is clear that an empty evening, one for which he has
nothing in his diary, actually worries him. Then he gets restless,

and goes from one haunt to another in search of company.

Bob's is by no means a ruined or a wasted life. He has had a fairly successful career in insurance; he has played a lot of golf; he has been involved in local council and on charity work. Those who have met him, and drunk with him, find him reserved but likable. He helps people and they appreciate it. But nobody feels that they know him.

The type of personality development that Bob represents reappears throughout Great Britain, in a number of variations. Not everyone who is like this went to a public boarding-school when very young, but the characteristics make sense in the context of Bob's experience.

He was forced to learn to keep his feelings under control to a degree that must be called unnatural for a young child. This undermined his ability to relate to others naturally. His father, on whom he had begun to rely, had died, and his mother—for reasons he scarcely understood—had sent him to this place where all his values in behaviour seemed to be turned upside down, and where the grown-ups demonstrably took little interest in an individual's personal problems. This is forcing self-reliance onto somebody with a vengeance. It is, in fact, tantamount to terrifying somebody out of the thought of relying emotionally on another human being again.

The substitute provided, and seized on by Bob, was to accept the large, impersonal, but impressive, organization as a pillar on which to lean. It is significant that he came to terms with his school, and was an 'establishment figure' inside it when he left: a prefect, in the first XV, active in several societies, including the Junior Training Corps. Then he made what seemed a logical progression through life: he joined the Navy; after that, a huge corporation. Working for a large political party could also be instanced as a further example of his need to be a cog in a wheel.

Society needs some people who will do this kind of thing, but it does not need people who can only do this kind of thing, and are unhappy without it. Children like Bob, when he was a child, should not be crammed into such a mould.

Three things in particular worked against him:

a Being sent to boarding-school when he was not mature enough, or adaptable enough, for it.

b Separation from mother, and sister, fairly soon after separa- from his father.

c Being sent to R, where young children like him were left to fend for themselves, in difficult circumstances.

Not all these factors by any means are working against all children who go to boarding-school but sometimes they do.

The fact that a large proportion of children who are felt to need to go to boarding-school come from homes where the parents have split up, or whose parents are living abroad, or are travelling continually, echoes the second factor. A recent survey suggested that about one in five boarding-school children come into this category. The younger a child is, the more likely he may be to be affected emotionally by a split in the home. But is it better, then, to risk emotional upset at a school, or to keep him at home, where he may be subject to strain, inadequate opportunity for education, etc.?

Miss P. has been a matron in charge of girls' boarding-houses for the past twenty-five years. She has worked in several different schools, and is in a position to draw conclusions about boarders from different backgrounds, as well as about boarders of different ages. Her conclusions are restricted to girls, but there is close agreement with observations from boys' schools.

Unless it is unavoidable, Miss P. believes, it is very unwise to send a girl to a boarding-school before she is eight years old. Up to that age, 'she needs love, and to be close to her mother: we can go some way towards helping them adjust to a boarding-school, once they are ready, but we cannot be substitute mothers'. Having said this, she admires the work she has seen done by some boarding-schools in caring for younger children, for whom the alternative would have been a very unsettled existence in a dis-integrating family. There is a part for boarding-schools to play here, she acknowledges, but it is an uphill struggle, which should be avoided if there is a choice.

For several years, Meg's parents prepared themselves for the time when they could separate permanently, without causing great havoc to their two children. Meg's brother George was two years older, and will be described later. Meg was felt by her parents to be the more difficult to make arrangements for. Partly because of her age, but also because she seemed more clinging, more sensitive, and more vulnerable, they felt that they ought to wait until she was eight before they sold their house, and separated. George had already been at boarding-school for three years. Now it was Meg's turn.

They decided that B was a good school academically, and that it had a happy atmosphere. Meg's mother herself had been to school there, and although there had been many changes in the intervening years, this was a reason to be optimistic.

Meg was all smiles when she arrived at B. The matron was agreeably surprised that here was someone who took to boarding very easily, without fuss, who joined in whatever was happening and got fun out of it. Meg was high-spirited, a bit mischievous, but always positive in what she did. She was popular too. Her first term was very happy.

The second term, after a holiday spent mostly with her mother, partly with her father, was very different. She had lost her enthusiasm. She had difficulties over her schoolwork, not so much through doing her work badly as by misunderstanding or forgetting what she was asked to do, losing books, and so forth. Her erstwhile popularity deserted her, and she had no particular friend. She took to teasing one of the girls in her dormitory, who was fat, and reduced her to tears several times.

The matron observed all this, and arranged meetings with Meg in her room, after school, at which she encouraged the girl to talk about what she was doing, and how she was feeling. Meg was at first very defensive with her, maintained that she was 'fine', and was not at all talkative. The matron avoided badgering her with questions. Instead, she talked about the other girls of her age. She intrigued Meg with a comment about a girl called Sally. From her observations of the children she knew that Sally too had no particular friend, and was close enough in interests to be likely to hit it off with Meg. She declared she was surprised Meg did not do more with Sally, since it was clear that Sally liked her. (Very soon she sowed a similar seed with Sally.)

Talking with Meg became easier from that moment, and when the matron said to her one evening, 'I expect you're looking forward to seeing your daddy this week-end', Meg was suddenly ready to unload everything.

Two things had coincided. The first was disillusion with boarding-school: it was not all wonderful, as her mother had implied. The second was awareness that all this talk of Mummy will be living here, and Daddy will be living there, because they feel better that way, was actually for *real*. The holidays had demonstrated this forcibly to her.

Meg seemed totally unaware that she had been at all unpleasant to the fat girl in her dormitory. The matron had often met similar cases, of a girl unable to express her difficulties and taking it out on another as though by a reflex action, without thinking.

Developing a friendship with Sally, and being able to talk about her anguish at not being able to be with both parents again, seemed to do Meg a lot of good. The matron kept an open invitation to Meg to talk more at any time. She never expressed great sympathy for Meg: experience taught her to discuss it with the child quietly, with a certain regret, but objectively, as though it were something on a table that they could approach as sensible people. She was also careful to avoid making any judgments for or against either parent. She has found this can be very difficult. Whenever Meg seemed to have talked enough at a particular session, she would turn the conversation towards Sally, or classroom projects, or a birthday party they were organizing for another child. This implied to Meg, over time—all right, your parents *are* getting divorced, and it's a shame, but meanwhile there are these other things in life, which are to be shared and enjoyed.

Meg's mother wanted to know how her daughter was, because on the telephone Meg had sounded distinctly blue. The matron used her discretion. By this time she was beginning to get through to Meg properly, and she felt reasonably confident. She reassured Meg's mother, on the grounds that this was the best thing for both parties.

Towards the end of the second term, Meg was much more cheerful. She had stopped being aggressive. She was on such good terms with Sally that she regretted having to part with her for the holidays. She still disliked the fact that her parents had split, but she had begun to accept it, as part of the fabric of her life.

Now, one year later, Meg is doing very well at school, and seems to be quite as happy as most of the other girls.

This need not have been the case. The matron tends to play down her own role in helping Meg to find her feet. She points out that Meg had obviously had 'a good upbringing', and had been given sound values about how to treat other people. Moreover, both parents clearly put themselves out to do their best by Meg, and she fully realized and returned their love. The matron has had other girls in her charge who have been much more difficult to help make happy.

The factors that she, and other matrons and teachers who were interviewed, regarded as likely to make things difficult for a young girl at boarding-school are shown below, in descending order of importance:

i   Family split—where the child is conscious of rejection by one or other parent; or, where the child is worried over tensions, the future, etc.

ii Awareness of partial rejection—of being tidied away into boarding-school for convenience.

iii Poor socialization, i.e. where a child is not used to getting on with other children, or dealing with new faces and experiences, unaccompanied by her parents. (Being an only child sometimes goes with this.)

iv Being separated from a brother or sister with whom she has been particularly close. (This applies to cases of family split, especially.)

v   Starting too young. (Opinions differ, but eight and nine are favoured ages for starting.)
vi Over-high expectations.

It will be noticed that Meg was partly, not wholly, affected by (i), and also by (vi). Interestingly enough, nearly all informants declared that intelligence, sensitivity, and physical fitness were all irrelevant to whether a child would enjoy boarding-school.

But even a casual set of visits to boarding-schools suggests that there are enormous differences in practice from one school to another. This must affect the chances of a successful boarding experience quite as much as anything else.

The most important example of this seems to come straight out of Meg's case history. Somebody at Meg's school made it her business to observe all the children in her care for signs of problems and signs of how to help them.

Rather different is this view, expressed by a matron at a different school, who had charge of girls in the same age range. 'They've got to learn to get along with each other, and I can't do it for them. . . . Some of them settle in quickly, and some of them wander about looking like sick cows. There's no accounting for children. But in nine cases out of ten, if there's trouble to begin with, they snap out of it sooner or later. The curriculum sees to that, you know. . . . They're missing their mummies at first. Well, they've got to learn to live without them. There's plenty to do, and I tell them to get on with it.'

It is worth examining these comments for words and phrases which signify compulsion: 'got to', 'snap out of it', 'sees to that', etc. It reveals a totally different approach. Many of the children at her school are enjoying themselves, to judge from the atmosphere. But for the odd ones out, the one out of ten who is conscious of separation, this could go hard. Meg's parents seem to have chosen the right school for their child.

Boys' boarding-schools greatly outnumber girls'. They are longer established, and in many of them there is a stronger feeling that traditional ways of doing things are a matter of pride. But here again, interviews with housemasters throw up a wide range of attitudes as to what kind of problems exist, and how they are best tackled.

The ultra-traditionalists are not dissimilar in what they say to the matron quoted above. Some of these declare that the organized religion of the school of itself resolves the personal problems of most of the younger entrants, but these are a minority.

At the other extreme are those who are anxious to experiment. Most of these aim at an ideal community that allows maximum individual expression consistent with a framework that protects the welfare of others, especially of those who are weaker. 'A kind of enlarged home, with lots of friends dropping in, and lots of ideas and things to do that you wouldn't normally find at home', is how one of these described what he was aiming at. Others in this group are eager to carry experiment further. For example: 'Quite frankly, most of our children's actual homes are ghastly places to be brought up in. Sometimes it's pressures, tensions, rows and divorce. But almost always there's this striving to be better than the next fellow; to get more money; to have a better job with more power; to win and never to lose. This is a bad way to begin life. Children nowadays need to break out of the family circle and do things in groups—for each other, not for themselves.' He encouraged the word 'commune', in situations where other educationalists might say 'family groups'—e.g. half a dozen children of different ages living and working as a unit, sharing their interests, and helping each other on projects.

There is an interesting similarity between these two extremes, the very traditionalist and the very progressive boarding-school, which both are liable to dispute. This is that if a young child is at a disadvantage to the others, and suffering from premature separation, neither school is anxious to take note of an individual's personal problems of adjustment if it means giving them more individual attention. Both will try to be nice to him, in their own way. But they are backing the *group* and the *organization* to sort out an individual's problems, by distracting him, involving him, and forcing him to think about other things. Schools that are between these two extremes will be more likely to be flexible towards individuals. They may be more prepared to probe beyond the minimal 'Well, Thompson, you seem to be finding the maths in 2B a bit sticky, and I'm told you don't exactly shine on the Rugby field—is there anything eating you?', to which the answer can only be, 'No, sir.'

Not all old schools are traditionalist in that way. Nor are all modern schools experimental to that point either: whether they are co-educational or not, whether they have thrown out school uniform is neither here nor there. The important points to look for are these:

a Is there any sign that the staff leave the needs of a young boy to be covered by a system, in which they have implicit faith? This could mean that they are abdicating personal responsibility for human communication.

b If they are flexible (i.e. (a) does not apply), do they have individual staff who give the impression that they really care about individual contact, enough to take the trouble to achieve it?

George

Meg's brother was lucky enough to go to a boarding-school that was satisfactory on both these points. Or rather, his parents were astute enough to find one.

Unlike Meg, he was not at all sure that he was going to like boarding-school when he arrived at his prep school, aged seven. He was, in fact, trying very hard to suppress the most lugubrious thoughts during his first week. 'Everything was so noisy,' he recalls, 'and everybody else seemed to know what to do, and I didn't.'

During this week he discovered that there were day boys, weekly boarders, and termly boarders in his school. Some terrible mistake had been made, he decided, in his case. They must be regarding him as a termly boarder, since he was in a dormitory for termly boarders. But had his parents really known that weekly boarding, or even day attendance, was possible? He seized his courage in both hands, apprehended the junior matron, who looked sympathetic, and—beetroot-faced—he exposed his theory that fate had blundered.

She laughed at him, to kill the false hope, but not unkindly. She took him in tow, along with another seven-year-old who seemed very much less than cheerful. 'I wonder if you could help me with the animals' cages,' she said. They were kept away from a homework session and taken into the junior classrooms, where there were hamsters, guinea-pigs and a rabbit. Some of these cages did not *need* cleaning: the principle was to get the boys involved, in a situation where she could open up conversation with them naturally, and privately.

Soon the two boys, who had been suspicious of each other's stony reserve, were each admitting frankly that they had already started to hate the place. The matron suggested that *lots* of the other boys felt the same ('They always do, at first'), but most of them were stubborn about admitting it. Knowing other boys, she put it to them, helps a lot, given time. It was difficult not to agree with her.

Soon the housemaster came in (by pre-arrangement) and asked them if they knew anything about dogs. His labrador needed exercise at the week-ends, and his son was having trouble building a kennel for him. Could they help? As a matter of fact, one was afraid of large dogs, and the other could not, as yet, hammer a nail in straight. But because they were appealed to directly in this way, they liked the feeling of being drawn in. And during that first week-end, they were encouraged to open up about what they did at home. George admitted to missing his sister, and mentioned the tree-house they had in their garden. He was not derided: he was told he could walk round and choose a site for a tree-house in the grounds. He talked about Meg, and felt better for doing so. His new friend was asked what he knew about the Persian Gulf, where his parents had gone at the behest of an oil company. They found the spot on the map and a project was set up to find out as much about the area as possible.

'Old Hawks' (as the housemaster is known) 'really made you feel that he wanted you to be there,' says George in retrospect. Now having the sophistication of a ten-year-old, he feels much more independent, and more resistant to a personal approach. But he likes the way he was treated at first, and describes the atmosphere as being rather like 'a crazy kind of family'.

*   *   *

Offering a mother-substitute, or a parent substitute, is unrealistic for a boarding-school except in a very watered-down sense. But offering a family substitute is not unrealistic. Those boarding-schools which treat children with sensitivity, and concern for their emotional development, can be distinguished by this characteristic.

Sheer lack of ritual, and the substitution of chaos for order, should not be mistaken for an attempt to have a family atmosphere. Young children are as likely to be alarmed by an absence of order as by a complex of rigid rules. This point is made with feeling by some of the most experienced and committed boarding-school people—in words like those of the more progressive hospital staff. Creating a family feeling demands hard work. It is very different from leaving everything to natural forces.

A one-sex school is, logically, a less normal environment than a co-educational school. One-sex boarding-schools predominate, however. Many who run, or work at, boarding-schools feel that this is wrong, and that for young children co-education would enhance the sensation of participating in an 'enlarged family'. The observation is also made that co-education is better for older children, from puberty onwards, in that it helps boys and girls to be less stilted in their approach to each other, more understanding, and more realistic in their expectations of each other.

The obstacles to those who want to turn their schools co-educational are partly economic and partly a matter of parental obstruction or disapproval by governing bodies. Change costs money, and most boarding-schools, being privately owned, find it daunting to plan for extra space and staff. State boarding-schools have, at present, a comparatively low priority when it comes to spending education budgets.

These points were taken into account by the Newsom Commission when they were examining the role that public schools could play in providing boarding-school places for the community at large. The commission's main anxiety was that there were many more children who had 'boarding need' than could be found places as things stood at present. 'One matter, however, is not in doubt. There are more children in need of boarding education than can receive it. . . . Children's Departments, already short of staff, are going to have to carry heavier burdens in future: children in "long-term care" frequently change foster homes and schools; their chances of academic success are correspondingly reduced, and very few of them go on to higher education. Boarding need is real.'

This is the view of a team of experts from various fields. It is significant for parents who, for one reason or another, want their young children to board: despite acknowledging what many critics have pointed out, they decided that boarding-schools fulfil a social need, and that at best they do this well.

The points made against boarding can be summarized as follows. Some apply to some schools more than to others. The list is intended so that parents can use it to judge schools for children boarding at an early age.

Is the school likely to:
a deprive them of individual interest and affection?
b force them to inhibit natural expression of their feelings?
c reduce contact with parents unnecessarily (i.e. restriction of phone calls, visits, etc., to a bare minimum)?
d deprive them of any basic privacy (e.g. are all baths communal? are there times at which they can choose to be by themselves, or with certain others, as opposed to being in large groups)?
e deprive them of any basic liberty (e.g. can they choose from a number of occupations at evenings and weekends? Can they read, go for a walk, practise the piano, go shopping . . .)?
f force them to eat food they dislike?

g mould them into organization men, to the point that confidence in their individual talents, and their ability to choose, atrophies?

h give them a sense of belonging to something so exclusive that when they leave they cannot adjust to reality, to the principle that other people are not inferior, or that the other sex is not dangerous?

i expose them to physical and mental bullying without taking measures against this?

No boarding-school is perfect. (Neither is any school.) Some perceptive boarding-school heads are able to judge that a particular boy, with a particular background, will do better in a particular boarding-house within his school. They realize that premature separation affects individuals differently, and that sometimes the appropriate house has to be chosen for the job.

Parents can do a lot to help their children when they go into boarding-school. In the first place, they scan the list of 'dangers' given above, in order to check periodically whether there are any signs of those dangers affecting their child's progress. In some cases they can counteract the effects. Where it is obvious a big mistake has been made, they should remove their child.

They should also ask themselves, where a really young child is concerned (say, under eight), or one who is older but not a strong character, or has been exposed to the tensions of a marital split, whether a weekly boarding arrangement is possible.

Here are other points that parents might remember, prior to their child's admission, and during the first term:

i Do not oversell the idea of boarding: making it seem like a wonder-world is very unfair, and over time (as with Meg) it is self-defeating.

ii Make sure they take something personal with them, that they are fond of and that will reassure them: a talisman, a collection, a toy—but if it is obtrusive (like Bob's teddy bear) make sure that his will not be the only one of its kind.

iii Once the decision is made that a child should go into such-and-such a school, arrange to make contact with him on a particular date, and stick to this unless the school advises to the contrary. Let him know what this date is to be, and show him on a calendar, or a diary, precisely when this means. The date should be about three weeks after entry. To come earlier, unexpectedly, will merely confuse and upset. It may also sour relations with the school, to no purpose.

iv Never break an appointment to ring up or visit the child. This undermines faith in the durability of the family despite the separation that boarding causes. Visit, and write, as regularly as possible.

v   Do not voice criticisms or anxieties about the school in the child's hearing. He may magnify them, and this makes your decision to send him there all the worse in his mind, quite apart from putting him off.

vi It is far from unknown for children to write down dramatic experiences of their plight, demanding release. The younger they are, and the more rudimentary the writing, the more pathetic it seems. Remember that this is a favourite means of letting off steam, which may sound far worse than is intended. If it continues it is definitely a sign that something is going wrong. In any event, the best course is to ring up, and talk things over first with the person in charge, next with the child. Airing complaints or doubts at an early stage is best, rather than bottling up your feelings until the situation becomes really emotional.

vii Some of the school's procedures and activities may strike you as unnecessary, or inane. Criticizing them soundly in front of the child is very unlikely to help him enjoy the school more. Try to show interest and ask intelligent quesions about those things which seem to attract the child's interest. You may dislike football, but to him it may be a life-line.

viii During term-time a boarder is missing out on family life. Make up for this during the holidays as much as possible. Try to restore his sense of family with a lot of conversation and a lot of shared activities.

ix Most boarders also miss out on neighbourhood friends,

children of the opposite sex, and children of other social strata during term-time. Anything to fill these gaps should be encouraged too.

x   An unexpected morale booster helps: for example, if the parents were living in Brussels, a telephone call from Belgium can be very exciting as well as reassuring.

Boarding-school is traditionally for the rich. The Newsom Commission, however, drew attention to the Ministry of Social Security's 1967 estimate of over 1.4 million children who were 'living in overcrowded conditions'. These may need boarding, for both educational and social reasons. The parents of most of them are very unlikely to be able to afford the cost.

Local education authorities can and do pay all the fees and most of the expenses involved in sending a child to a boarding-school. For this, application has to be made directly to them, and each case is judged on its merits. Anyone who feels strongly that their child should have the opportunity of boarding-school, but cannot afford it, could ring their L.E.A. officer and ask who they should be talking to about this, and what details they should provide. The criterion that the L.E.A. follows in deciding whether a case has been fully made out, is to see whether any of the following applies:

a Specialized education, or educational treatment is needed. (For example, an autistic child needs specialist teachers to develop his full potential: there are few such units in the country. Similarly, some children with special aptitudes (e.g. for music) may need education at a boarding-school specializing in music.)

b There is no suitable education near home. ('Suitable' means right for that child; 'near' depends on transport availability rather than distance.)

c The child needs to be taken into care, into a foster home or an institution.

Authorities vary in the way that they interpret whether they should pay for boarding education in 'borderline' situations.

113

These can include circumstances where parents travel a great deal; where getting to the nearest State school is difficult but possible, on a daily basis; and where the suitability of the local schools is in dispute. But bearing these points in mind, if you feel you have a good case, make it out—strongly.

Nine
Mental Handicap and
Mental Disturbance

One of the most agonizing decisions that parents may have to make is whether a handicapped child should live separately from them or at home. There are usually plenty of arguments to be made, for and against both courses of action. Professional advice is often important, to help parents understand the nature of the child's condition, and what kind of development is possible. But professional people often disagree, and parents may have to consider and choose between alternative opinions and advice. In the last resort, they will recognize that their child is not just a mongol, or aphasic, or schizophrenic. He is John, or Jane, and is just that bit different from the others who may be given the same description, in ways that are important. He has a particular relationship with his family, whether he is deeply affectionate or seemingly indifferent. These things matter when it comes to deciding how best to help him, and the family as a whole.

This is not a book in which to find out about diagnosis; that is a professional task. But before discussing some of the important aspects of arrangements involving separation, some distinctions have to be drawn. 'Mental handicap' covers an enormous area. It covers cases, for example, where a child has a learning problem but seems to be absolutely normal in emotional terms. It covers other cases where there is a complex of emotional and behavioural disturbance that makes it difficult to know where the condition starts and where it ends. There are cases where there is a clear-cut physical reason for the child's condition: for example, a child may be deaf, and may have developed behavioural problems in an attempt to come to terms with the world he finds extremely difficult to understand. There are others where the cause is obscure, and authorities disagree, for example, whether a child's emotional difficulties put him off learning, or whether it is the other way round.

'Mental disturbance' is usually used to indicate a condition where a child would be normal were it not for a serious psychological problem setting in. There are no—or at least no visible—physical causes for it. The child's sense of reality, and of what is important and unimportant may become quite unbalanced in these cases. Or there may be normal mental and emotional development apart from certain morbid fears, or obsessions. Some cases have been the subject of dispute for many years. For example, a child with schizophrenic symptoms will be considered by some experts to have a defect in the chemistry of his brain, and by others to have been subject to a serious shock in early infancy of a mental, not a physical, kind.

There are many children who will not fit neatly into any of these categories. Some may become easier to diagnose when they grow older. If separation is being considered, it is best to have a reasonably well-formed idea of the category that a child is more likely to be in, even if it is impossible to be precise. This is because the effects of separation can be markedly different, depending on what is wrong with him, and on whether appropriate training and teaching are going to be provided for him, and for his condition.

Diagnosis, then, is the first real hurdle. Obviously, in severe cases where a child is clearly a mongol, or has cerebral palsy, specialist help should have been involved from the beginning. It is the cases where a child seemed to be normal at birth, and in his development up to about a year, before lagging behind or becoming odd in behaviour, that diagnosis can become a long-drawn-out struggle. Doctors vary a lot on whether they advise parents to wait until a child is older before taking him to see a specialist. Those who say, 'Be patient and wait', dislike suggesting to a child that he may be different from others, or they suspect that the parents are fussing, and not making allowance for different rates of progress among normal children. Some doctors also have a suspicion that psychiatrists too may make too much of idiosyncrasies.

Some very young children are very difficult to diagnose, and this has to be put off. But there seems little harm in getting a specialist to do the putting off, rather than a local G.P., who has admittedly seen a great number of children but lacks specialized knowledge. If a parent is seriously worried that her G.P. is not tackling the problem as quickly as it deserves, there is no reason why she should not insist on getting an introduction to a specialist. Seeing a specialist is a right under the National Health Service. If the local doctor is adamant, she can go to the local Child Guidance Clinic, or make contact with the Health Officer who probably visited her when the child was still an infant, and will be in a position to assess progress. It is an unfortunate fact that a visit to a psychiatrist can often be arranged more quickly on a private basis than under the Health Service. This applies to other specialists too, and there are a number of these who may need to be seen—to check for deafness, for example. This is why arranging a visit to the consultant paediatrician at a major hospital can save a lot of time: he can, if he sees fit, arrange for a series of specialized tests to be done relatively quickly.

One advantage of an early diagnosis—provided it is soundly based and made by a competent authority—is that plans can start to be made soon. It also means that the parents themselves are spared a great deal of mental strain, which inevitably attends a period of 'Is he, or isn't he?'

There are some conditions for which provision of specialized teaching methods seems to make a lot of difference to the amount of useful learning, and therefore of self-sufficiency, that a child eventually achieves. This is true, for instance, in the case of autism. But the number of schools, or units within schools, that can provide this for autism, or for a number of other handicaps, is severely limited. Those which offer residential care as well as teaching tend to have long waiting lists. This goes for many day schools too. Applications then need to be made quickly—as soon as parents have a clear idea of where to apply. All in all, the case for pressing to get an interview with a specialist, provided parents are clear in their minds that something is wrong with their child, seems very strong.

In some cases parents can be told with some accuracy what sort of prognosis to expect. If they have a mongol child they will be told what sort of attainment he is capable of reaching. (Mongol children sometimes produce happy surprises, and can achieve more independence than used to be expected, but broad goals can be reasonably set.) Other children may be much more difficult to assess in this way. Where there is obvious brain damage, the full extent to which this may be compensated for may be open to question.

This is tied in with the problem of whether it may be better for the child to be in a residential school, or to live at home, and at what age. There is more knowledge about well-studied groups like mongols so that their reactions on separation can be planned for too. Others may not seem to follow any kind of generalized rule about how they react. It may depend on whether they are going through a period of particular dependence on one individual, as much as on their condition.

Societies formed to protect the interests of handicapped children of various types are often in the best position to advise on this. They can sometimes sum up the way in which a particular child and a particular school seem likely to fit together, where a specialist may not be able to unless he has a special concern with one abnormal group. These societies vary to some extent in the service that they provide, but they will nearly always advise on possible schools, or residential homes. The most comprehensive of them, the National Society for Mentally Handicapped Children, has people with a wide range of experience, which it can bring to bear for the aid of any handicapped child. It is no bad plan, particularly if there is an element of doubt in a child's diagnosis, to start with the NSMHC, then apply as well to a specialist society for further help. A list of some of the main societies of this kind will be found at the end of this book.

Occasionally it happens that a couple despairs of their mentally handicapped child ever achieving anything worth while. They despair too of being able to live happily with him. They accordingly abandon him. This is the extreme form of premature separation. Mental hospitals know it as 'dumping'.

Tim was 'dumped', when he was three. M hospital has several children like him, who underwent a similar experience. His parents arrived one afternoon at visiting time, and stopped a nurse on a staircase. 'This little kiddie's wandering all by himself,' said the father, gesturing to Tim. The nurse saw a bemused little boy who had difficulty in walking, whined, and was plainly dressed in a blue jersey and jeans, with gym shoes. Clearly, she thought, he must be one of ours. 'Oh! where did you find him?'

The mother pointed up to the landing at the top of the stairs. 'He nearly fell down, so we thought we ought to take him back up.'

The nurse said she had better find out about him—and led Tim upstairs. By the time she discovered that he was not known in any of the wards, his parents had gone. An attempt was made to trace them, but when it became obvious that this would be very difficult if not impossible, the search was called off. They have never reappeared.

Tim is called Tim because the ward sister to whose care he was allotted liked the name, and she had no other Tim around to confuse her.

Nobody is quite sure what is wrong with him. It is clear that he has some brain damage, which makes his muscle control awkward, and which is presumably the cause of his lack of speech. Now five, he has some oddities, such as a habit of rubbing his cheek against the windows, which can keep him happy for a long time. But he is by no means a difficult child in the ward. He doesn't molest any other children, and he complies with what the staff want him to do. Occasionally he has a tantrum, and howls and screams, but this is rare. (He may even do this less often than a normal child.) He is not destructive, although being a bit clumsy with his hands he sometimes breaks toys accidentally. This makes him angry with himself, and sad.

It is impossible to tell what might have been had Tim remained with his parents. If they had despised him, or ignored him, quite possibly he would not have come on at all: he might even have been worse off. But here are some pointers, indicating what separation meant for him.

When he was left at M hospital, he was rather on the plump side. Clearly, he had been used to eating well. For his first six weeks in hospital he pined—refusing all food, all drink. He was given glucose injections until he was coaxed back into eating by having chocolate bars slipped into his mouth when not expecting it. He did not want to do anything: when led out of bed, he made for a corner of the ward, under a bed, and stayed there until brought out forcibly. He hated the noise that one of the other children made, and sometimes sat for a long time with his hands over his ears. It is possible that he may not have been responsive to his parents at all, but there is no doubt that his new life was mostly hateful to him, for a long time.

During the past two and a half years, Tim has not learnt a great deal. He lends a hand sometimes when he is being dressed, but he cannot do this job for himself. He has a few meaningful sounds, which suggest 'No!', 'More!' and 'I want that!' There are no recognizable words, however. His biggest achievement is that he can now push down his trousers and his pants and urinate into a pot when he needs to. He prefers his own company to that of the other children. Sometimes he seems to copy something that they do, but mostly he is fixed in his habits, such as rubbing the windows. It is difficult to guess how much language he can understand: he certainly responds to some of the nurses' instructions, but it is doubtful whether this is more than a set of reactions to specific situations.

'He probably would be learning a lot more,' the consultant felt, 'if he had more individual attention. At M we are over-crowded, as you can see, and there is about one permanent staff to twenty children. There are two classrooms, in which a number of selected children of five and over are given lessons. There has to be selection, because the school unit is too small not to have to concentrate its efforts on those who seem the most likely to benefit.' So far, Tim hasn't been lucky enough to go to school.

No one is likely to foster or adopt Tim. He does get visits from the Friends of M Hospital, who make it their practice to visit the children who get no other visits—approximately one in four at M hospital. Each of these gets roughly one personal visit a month. He is brought a cake on his 'official' birthday too; and he is included in the outings they organize, usually twice a year.

So much for personal contact, in a ward where the staff changes regularly, and there is often not enough manpower to open the toy cupboards, or to take the children into the grounds on warm sunny days. (Clearing up and supervision are too time-consuming.) It should, however, be stressed, that there was much less personal contact with children ten years ago, before the present consultant took over.

One bright spot is that the headmistress of a nearby girls' school has begun arranging for some members of her fifth and sixth forms to undertake regular visiting of some of the younger children. Perhaps one of them may be attracted by Tim's face, or feels that she likes his name.

It looks as though Tim's future lies in one of the wards for adolescents. It takes courage to go into some of these. Not because M hospital is unusual, unkind, or workshy. It is simply overloaded, and will continue to be so until society changes its priorities and puts up enough money to help children to transfer out of institutions instead of equipping many of them for little better than progress from one ward to another as they get older. The adolescent wards are characterized by a sense of a battle being gradually lost through lack of an army. Some go to lessons, and some have hobbies that they can get on with. Some are beginning to make themselves useful in the tiny workshop, and in the gardens. But most of them spend most of every day in, on, or around their beds. They sometimes fight, because they are bored, but they are not often unpleasant to each other. Visits are fewer, possibly because the children are less 'nice' as they grow older. It is alarming, at first, to see some of them strapped down so that they cannot masturbate to fight off boredom: they usually request this, because they have discovered that they hurt themselves by doing it too often.

It is unlikely that Tim's parents thought out precisely what they were doing when they abandoned him. If they had, it would have been unrealistic to expect anything better.

*   *   *

There are not many who are so calculating and deceitful in the way they dump a child. Many more cast around for a suitable home, a place which will take the child off their hands but treat him well, and prepare him for a happy and useful life, as far as is possible. Later, finding how difficult this can be, they settle for a place that does not quite measure up. They have their freedom, but they have a sense of failure too. Eventually, paying visits, only to have that failure underlined in their minds, is more agonizing than they can accept. Reluctant to try to find a better solution, they abandon him. Hospital almoners and social workers can call them back, once or twice—but not for regular contact, once despair has set in.

This is tragic in every sense. The parents themselves have suffered a lot and deserve consideration. But they do not understand how dependent a handicapped or disturbed child can be on keeping this association alive. Hospital staff can usually see the effect of visits stopping on a child who seems to respond very little but still expects them. The visits themselves may seem futile: blank incomprehension from the child, perhaps, with just a few telltale signs that certain gestures and certain people are recognized. But stop them and in some cases there is severe withdrawal, the child apparently losing whatever skills he has begun to learn.

Possibly the worst aspect of dumping, though, is that it influences the mentality of future generations. At a time when the official policy is to phase out large hospitals for the mentally handicapped and the mentally ill, and to organize care and treatment based on the community, the dumping attitude is calculated to keep conditions firmly in the nineteenth century. The other children, and the friends of the dumpers, must be affected by the implications that this is what is done with abnormal children. Normal life is for normal people, they will believe, and

subnormal people should be looked after elsewhere. After all—
we pay rates and taxes for it, don't we?

But Tim, and those like him, can make far more progress if they
are given encouragement, patience, example, and personal
attention. Normal children are 'stretched' to their advantage (if
it is not done to excess), by contact with older children, whether
this is in the schoolroom or the recreation ground. Second and
third children in a family often learn by imitating the first
children. The same principle applies to most handicapped or
disturbed children. They need examples, at least part of the time,
of normal behaviour, normal skills and normal relationships.
Children who are offered nothing but the sight of those who are
more handicapped or disturbed than they are will regress not
progress.

When parents feel that for very good reasons their child needs
to live somewhere else, this is one point they must check on, and
later reassess: what opportunities are there for their child to be
'stretched'? Will he be likely to pick up, partly through
specialized training, partly through the example of others, some
behaviour, and some learning that will make regular visiting
more a matter of pride and happiness, and less of a chore
dictated by conscience?

These criteria are not easy to satisfy.

When a child is severely handicapped, and the pressures on the
parents of limited space, limited money, limited time to look
after him, and the demands of the rest of the family combine to
make it impossible for him to stay at home, the local authority
is asked through the office of the Children's Officer, to find somewhere suitable. There are two broad alternatives, which in many
areas may be reduced to one. There are mental sub-normality
hospitals, which take children long-term (at least for as long as
it takes these hospitals to be 'phased out', as policy now urges),
and provide care, but not necessarily treatment. There are also
psychiatric hospitals, which vary in the length of time they take
children, and provide treatment, as well as care. It follows that those
children who are considered more likely to respond to treatment
will tend to be moved to psychiatric hospitals. But, both because

diagnosis is sometimes arguable, and because hospitals are not always true to type, and because of the limitations of space within catchment areas, very similar children may be found in both. The catchment area principle means that parents living within a particular local authority's borders may not have any choice, depending on the number of hospitals serving that authority's needs. This would be fine if all hospitals were the same and offered the same things. Emphatically, they are not. To be able to exercise choice a parent may need to gain entry for his child into a *specialist* hospital (or a hospital with a specialist unit); and show to the satisfaction of the local authority that this is a more suitable place for him, on treatment or educational grounds. The only other way is to consult with a specialist children's society—many have comprehensive files on hospitals with up-to-date information on standards of care and treatment reported by their members—and make the decision to move home, to live in a better catchment area.

Ken

For several years Ken, who is mongol, and just about average in terms of ability, had been attending a local training-centre. A coach organized by the council collected him from the door every morning, and brought him back in the afternoon, about four o'clock. The training centre provided a varied diet of elementary formal teaching for those who could benefit from it; useful hints on roads, cars, traffic lights, pedestrian crossings, and the desirability of holding hands; and play, in which constructional toys were used by way of preparation for training in the workshop. Whenever Ken's mother visited the centre she was pleased at the happy atmosphere, and the way the organizer tried to ensure that there was something for everyone to enjoy at some part of the day.

By the time he was nine, Ken had learnt to recognize words like 'Danger', and was reasonably easy to keep clean. He gave warnings about needing the lavatory, even though he could not be relied on to cope with the problems entirely by himself. He was a big boy, however, growing large and strong. As he grew more boisterous, he became more difficult to control. His mother was a frail woman, and she had a five-year-old to look after as well. There was absolutely no malice in Ken's naughtiness, but it was trying, for all that. This year, and next year, his mother calculated, she would be able to control him when he wanted to kiss the lady in the sweet shop. But he was growing bigger, and she was not.

Had her husband not died it would certainly have been easier for her. She had a sister, with a large young family, who could scarcely be expected to help a great deal, and one or two other relatives who were not anxious to volunteer. The Child Guidance Clinic advised her that Ken was probably old enough to benefit from a residential school. They pointed out that he could be helped, at the right school, to develop sound habits that were proving difficult for her to teach him.

The problem was to find a suitable school. The clinic put her name down, but could not say when a place would become vacant. The local NSMHC branch gave her the names of several places that they felt would suit Ken. They were likely to be full to the brim, they advised, but because of her particular circumstances, if she approached them personally, one or two might be able to slip Ken in front of the queue.

Private schools, of course, can use their discretion where entrance is concerned. One of them, in the West Country, took Ken on from the beginning of the following term. The local authority felt that this would be entirely right for him, and since there was nowhere more suitable at hand they agreed to bear the total costs. This included, after a means test, provision for Ken's mother to visit her son during his first term.

She took him to stay for a week-end in a little town near the school, during the holidays. They were allowed (in fact, encouraged) to visit the school several times, and show Ken the room in which he was going to sleep. All this probably meant less to Ken than, say, paying a preliminary visit to a boarding prep-school means to a normal five-year-old, but the school sets great store by careful introduction to minimize distress.

Ken settled down happily, very quickly. He has made a lot of progress. While his reading, his writing, and his use of numbers may seem the most dramatic of his new achievements, his mother is particularly grateful for his social improvements. There are certain things, like tidying his bedroom, that she had practically despaired of getting him to do. Sometimes a child refuses to learn things from his parents but will accept instruction in them from others. This, she discovered, applies to handicapped as well as to normal children.

Three points are worth emphasizing. The first is that in this case, Ken's mother and possibly his sister would have suffered considerably had Ken remained at home. Having him back in the holidays means hard work, but he is easier since he has been away to school, and knowing that term-time follows holiday-time helps make the task enjoyable. The second is that Ken was able to benefit positively from this particular school because it is one that believes in teasing out a child's ability, in giving him confidence and in getting handicapped children of different kinds to live with and help each other, under the close eye of a house mother. The third point is that, although she had good help from her local clinic and from the NSMHC, there were certain things she had to do for herself. She had to find out about schools, visit them, make applications, plead, and organize Ken's introduction to the school—*herself*.

Maralyn

Various things went wrong when Maralyn was little. Her father walked out, and her stepfather, although not outwardly cruel, wanted as little to do with her as possible. She was also one of a number of children involved in a train accident when she was three. She had only cuts and bruises when she was lifted clear from the wreckage, but the experience was harrowing: her mother in fact believes that she has never been *quite* the same since the crash, although she had always been an anxious child who cried easily.

She went into her local primary school at five and a half. For a year nothing very unusual about her was noted at school, except that she was shy and rather unresponsive. In her second year the difference between her work and the others' was more marked. She had difficulty in finishing anything. When she did, it was usually a repetition of a simple pattern, instead of the set task. Instead of an animal in the trees she might produce a whole lot of semi-circles. When questioned she wouldn't actually talk about her drawing, except to say, 'It's all right, isn't it?' If pressed to say where the animal was, and which were the trees, she would laugh, a bit hysterically, and tear it all up. She seemed to be wanting the others to laugh too and recognize that her work was just a joke. Her school friends tended to find her rather peculiar, and difficult to get on with.

At the teacher's suggestion she was taken to the psychologist at the local Child Guidance Clinic, who recommended that a psychiatrist should see her. On the basis of this report a place was sought for her at a unit for disturbed and maladjusted children, at an ESN school for Educationally Sub-normal children that served the district.

There were problems with her mother, who accepted that her daughter was 'not much good at learning', but felt that she did not deserve the stigma—as she saw it—of going to an ESN school. The stepfather took the view that a lot of fuss was being made about nothing.

Maralyn, according to the psychologist, was suffering continual alarms from two sources. The first was that her parents were fed up or dissatisfied with her, and the second was an aspect of school life that is sometimes missed by parents: anything that the class was asked to do of a complicated nature terrified her. It was not understanding that was difficult so much as overcoming the alarm that began when teacher started saying, 'Now listen to this, all of you. . . .' If spoken to directly, however quietly and kindly, she at once concentrated on getting out of the situation—for example, by nodding vigorously and saying, 'Yes, miss!' She eluded observation by copying the others, as far as she could. Viewed in this light, her achievements at school had to be called impressive rather than poor.

Some of this made sense to her mother, when carefully explained, because it was not unlike Maralyn's behaviour with her stepfather. When she talked with the teacher in charge of the unit for disturbed children, she was impressed with her as a person, and she agreed to Maralyn's going there.

Maralyn was singled out by the psychologist as a perfect example of a child who should certainly not be sent away to a residential school. She is extremely nervous of the outside world, and what it has to offer. She is already a practised hand at evading attention from adults, and even from other children. Her mother is the one person with whom she feels at all capable of relaxing. For her to find herself suddenly cut off from her mother, and surrounded by strange demands, would be a very bad shock.

At the moment, she is progressing much more satisfactorily than she had alone at the primary school. Being in a class of ten means that her teacher can devote a good deal of time to coaxing her into treating everything more naturally, with more confidence. When she is older, and emotionally more stable, she might possibly benefit from a boarding-school of a specialized kind, seeing that her home life is not ideal. But separation has to be some years off.

* * *

This may give an entirely mistaken impression, that disturbed children should not be separated, while mentally handicapped children can be sent to boarding-school. It is much more a matter of assessing individual children's needs. For example, simply because a young child seems to be unhappy at home is no reason to suppose that she may not suffer more away from it. Analysing the rights and wrongs of this is a skilled professional job, because it means uncovering, painstakingly, just what home and the people in it mean to a particular child. Some parents are suspicious of psychiatrists: but if psychiatrists did not exist, someone would have to try to help disturbed children by making a special study of them, and he would be called a psychiatrist.

Brothers and sisters can be very much affected by growing up with a handicapped child. What is sometimes not appreciated, however, is that the influence is often for good. If they find they have to be careful with their handicapped brother or sister, so as not to hurt him, and play with him, they become more understanding of other people's feelings, and more considerate. This is not to say that other children do not share these traits, but other writers have noted how sensitive and mature the brothers and sisters of handicapped children seem to be. This can go too far, however, when harassed parents pass on the responsibilities of looking after a severely handicapped child down the family: this can rob a child of time in which he should be feeling carefree, and being 'stretched' by playing more complex games with older children. Trying to preserve a proper balance can be difficult, particularly if parents fall ill.

This has prompted the idea that it is sometimes better for the normal child in a family to go away to boarding-school. For part of the year, then, he would be free of concern for the handicapped child, and would appreciate his company the more during the holidays. But the normal child must not be given to understand that it is because of his handicapped brother that he is being sent away. This can provoke immediate resentment, particularly if the separation occurs before the child is mature enough to take it in his stride. With this important proviso, and bearing in mind the general strictures about boarding-schools made in the preceding chapter, it is a tactic that could be very useful. Getting money from local authorities to cover boarding fees for the normal child in the family is rare but not unknown. A doctor would need to make out a strong case for this, on the basis of the health or mental health of the normal child being in jeopardy.

There are extreme cases where a handicapped child (but more often a disturbed child) is liable to cause serious physical harm to a normal brother or sister. This is indeed a harrowing situation. The alternatives seem to be to mount a twenty-four-hour guard, or to send the handicapped child away immediately, without being able to reconnoitre a suitable home for him. The recently introduced Attendance Allowance was intended to help here. Every parent of handicapped or disturbed children who need special attention at all times should make inquiries at the local office of the Department of Health and Social Security, whether they might be entitled to the money. This will defray at least some of the cost of keeping a severely handicapped child at home. But this can only be a very small part of the answer. In the past, when there were large family units, in large living spaces, coping with such a child was easier. Opportunities for sharing the burden through the family should be investigated, nevertheless.

It is less fashionable for grandparents to live in, but it can be a great help. Meanwhile, the effort to find appropriate training for the handicapped child—which may be at, or away from, home, possibly on a weekly basis—must go on.

Some parents are shy, or proud, about telling a social worker at the Child Guidance Clinic all about the background problems. These may include lack of money, unemployment, or the need for the mother to be employed because of the husband's unemployment, stress caused to others in the family, and having to move home. This is a shame, because although social workers cannot work miracles they are paid to find out how best to help people, and to find ways of achieving this.

When a handicapped brother or sister is taken into care, or placed in a residential home or school, a normal child sometimes feels more regret than may appear on the surface. Prior to this he may have complained of roughness, or embarrassment aroused by his brother. Afterwards, he may feel guilty, and will almost certainly miss him. He should be brought in on visits, provided the parents are satisfied that the scene in a ward will not be harrowing for him, and he should help with treats and surprises for his brother whenever he returns home for a spell.

The comment made under Long-Stay in Hospital applies here as well: there is enormous variation among the places to which a handicapped child may be sent. It is even more difficult to make a good choice, perhaps, and because there has to be some specialized training for a child with a special handicap if he is to improve. These are two points that parents can look for, during their anxious and sometimes demoralizing search for the right spot:

1 People are more important than space or facilities. Is there one (or more) person there, in whom the parents have real confidence from the point of view of making contact with their child, and making real use of that contact?

2 The immediate group which a handicapped or disturbed child is to join will be very important in helping him to become a more aware and a more sociable person. What is that group like? Does it include some who are in the same age bracket, and some who are at a similar level of handicap? (Different *sorts* of handicap within the group need not in itself be a drawback—in fact, some, e.g. the Rudolf Steiner schools, claim it is an advantage. It is a question of whether the children are at complementary stages, and can help each other.)

Many of the other points to look for are covered in the advice given at the end of the Long-Stay in Hospital chapter. One deserves to be singled out: is there a feeling that a child is encouraged to be an *individual*, with his own possessions clearly at hand, and his own insignia on a cupboard or a wall? Awareness of oneself as a separate, competent and noteworthy individual is an important and sometimes very difficult stage for these children. A normal child, staying in a hospital for a long period, needs to have his sense of individuality protected: a handicapped or disturbed child usually needs to have his built.

One of the things that parents, especially mothers, resent about looking after handicapped children at home is the way they are treated by other parents. Society as a whole shuns the abnormal: it would be so much nicer, it feels, if these mongol children with their distinctive faces, and these others without speech, or without normal emotions, were kept to one side, so that they did not have to be regarded. Quite clearly they are a source of fear, since they remind people that they too for no apparent reason might have such a child—or even have *been* such a child. They know nothing about how very delightful an NSMHC party can be; or the tremendous bond of affection that can be built within a family for a mongol, or an autistic, or many other kinds of outlaw child. Nor do they know, as they worry about their children's common entrance exams or 'O' levels, how enormously proud a parent can feel when his handicapped child speaks his first spontaneous sentence. Still less do they imagine it possible that handicapped children have themselves drawn magnificent pictures, written stories, and passed 'O' levels.

Knowing that other parents feel sorry for you, invite you less often, steer their children away from yours, is an experience that gives you a tough hide. Not all neighbours or friends will practise avoidance in this way. Those who do not are to be treasured. That people should take a more liberal view of accepting handicapped children in the community is vitally important for their future. This is because the official policy of substituting hospitals for them with hostels, within the community (giving them a better chance both of treatment and integration), depends for its implementation on provisions made by local authorities. These have to take over, adapt, plan and build hostels. For them to do this quickly, and on a sufficient scale, depends in turn on their view of local feeling about the priority to put on this activity, and the extent of reaction towards paying more, in order to help these children live close to, and among the rate-payers. Despite government aid, rates are bound to go up.

One recent experience in a city in the Midlands inspires doubt about this. The local branch of the National Society for Autistic Children bought a large house on the understanding they would get permission to adapt it for use as a small school, on a combined day and residential basis, starting with about twelve children. This was in a middle-class residential suburb. The very idea of such children being taught, and playing in a garden, in close proximity to theirs, was enough to start a petition among nearby residents against planning permission. They probably did not know what autistic children were like, in many cases. They certainly did not want to find out. In fact, the scheme went through, and the residents now realize it does not affect them one scrap.

Some hostels exist already. In some cases, hostels have been built, or adapted, for older as well as for young handicapped people. Many authorities have hostel provision in their plans for future work. The speed with which they and educational facilities are developed for these children depends very much on public opinion. In the meantime parents who really need to have their handicapped child looked after away from home must examine cautiously the provision that is offered locally: if this seems to be wrong for their child, in the light of the professional advice they have received, and of their own observations, they face anxious negotiation. To be successful in this, and find the right place for their child, they will need a sympathetic ear at the local authority; long discussions with one or more of the children's societies; a lot of visits to specialist units, State and private residential schools, and the like; a lot of waiting, and probably some arguing; pertinacity; and luck.

Ten
What can a Parent do
about Separation?

Some children, when all is said and done, are demonstrably more capable of dealing with a strange or frightening situation than others. These differences are large, even at a very early age, as many objective nurses in hospitals will verify. While heredity may have some part to play in this, it seems unrealistic not to think of how some children's backgrounds and upbringing contribute towards making them more secure when it comes to separation.

One important point stems from the proposition put forward in the first chapter: that a major separation experience should, if possible, be prepared for by careful extension of a child's experience. This may involve mini-separations: these are not advocated for their own sake, but for the chance they provide of letting a child understand that he can rely on and derive interest and pleasure from other people. This extension should, ideally, start in a small way, at an early age, for just part of a day. The period can be lengthened, and the time of day varied, according to evidence that the child accepts it. In many homes this happens naturally. It does not take great organization, except where a mother or another relative is forced to cope on her own. Eventually longer periods than a day will be tolerated. If a mother has to go back to work, with the child still very young, it helps if this is established by stages, from part-time to full-time, and then within a recognizable routine.

There is more to it than this, however. Children value reliability. There is something very reassuring about having a special degree of contact at a particular time, such as bed-time. A parent who gives the time, not necessarily for very long, regularly and unreservedly to a child will be regarded as reliable. That is, even when there is some form of separation. A parent who seems to have phases of being 'on' the child, or 'off' the child, is automatically less reliable. The child is readier to put a bad construction on a separation situation.

The importance of touching and cuddling has been stressed by psychologists in recent years, as being central to personality development. One aspect of touching is that, apart from being an obvious reassurance about love between mother and child, it provides evidence of return by the mother to the child, from whatever activity she was involved in. Reappearing in a room and saying 'Hello!' is fine as far as it goes. This does not make the mistake of rushing in and saying, 'Are you all right, then?', which is self-defeating because it over-dramatizes separation. But a quiet hug indicates that it was important for the mother to come back as opposed to being simply part of her schedule.

Many mothers are suspicious of others' approaches to their children when they are very small. Some resent it. Some are convinced that nobody understands or can handle their infant as they can. In a sense, they are right. But it is a shortsighted attitude, if it means screening a child from the experience of other hands feeding him, dressing and undressing him, and other voices talking to him. A child who is exposed to other children, and a range of friendly adult faces (provided the situation is under control), will gain a wider repertoire of behaviour to deal with the unexpected. Children with nursery school experience, for example, are as a rule found by primary school teachers to be more mature in socialization, as well as educationally. They also have an advantage when a separation is forced on them.

One theory is that before the Industrial Revolution individual family units were less watertight. Families intermingled, on a district or village basis, and children were accepted in and out of several homes, relatively freely. This ended when people were packed into narrower space, in industrial areas. Everybody in a locality no longer knew everybody, and doors became closed. Through the Victorian period, the size of families, and the tendency to keep grandparents, aunts, etc., under the same roof, meant that young children still had varied experience of attention and handling. But in the twentieth century, the process of compartmentalization of nuclear family units has continued, until reaching the ultimate in cell-block planning as represented by high-rise flats—where some sociologists have found drastically little social interchange between children, or adults. Apart from architectural discouragement to interchange, the smaller the family unit the more tired the parents get (especially if they both have a hard job), which makes an 'open house' arrangement for children undesirable.

Some parts of the United Kingdom seem somehow to have preserved a sense of local community. This does not mean the occasional fête, or contrived coffee morning: it means people coming and going, uninvited, as the fancy takes them, or as they have a particular need for help, or a talk. This is somewhat contrary to Anglo-Saxon convention, but an attempt to move back in this direction would certainly benefit our children.

Anxiety is very easy to communicate. It seems unfair to recommend parents not to worry overtly when a separation situation is imminent. For many it is impossible advice. But it is worth reflecting how alarming certain trigger-words can be, when overheard by a young child. Some nurses say they cringe when a mother tactlessly asks, in front of a three-year-old, something like, 'Does the doctor think his wound is still infected?' Even a sick child will read more than you suspect into your mood and your words.

As children get older they inevitably try things which parents can foretell will end in frustration, and perhaps a bruised knee. Rescuing a child from danger is obviously the first priority. Warning them that 'You'll never do that!' when they try a handstand on the grass makes no sense whatever. Offering a helping hand is all right—not too urgently. Letting them get on with it gets them used to trying out new things. Sometimes they succeed, sometimes they fail—perhaps painfully. Discovering this is a pre-condition to becoming resilient, and it has to be done alone

Once a child obviously has suffered from premature separation —what then? There is a great deal that parents can do.

At child guidance clinics, one of the most frequent comments on case studies is this: 'As soon as his mother accepted the fact that her child had been seriously disturbed by the separation, the family started to make some progress.' Whether or not a mother, or a father for that matter, was in fact responsible for the separation—be it a walk-out, or getting the child received into care during an illness, or whatever—there is often a feeling that it was somehow their fault. This is a bar to admitting the importance of the event, particularly if it happened long before. But both parents have to face the reality of premature separation trauma, if anything really relevant is going to be done by way of reconstruction.

What has happened is an interruption of a crucial relationship. Strengthening this bond is the best course. This is not always possible, in which case a bond with a substitute figure is needed.

This is a convenient point at which to mention a form of separation that is irrevocable: death of the mother, or the father. There is a school of thought, particularly in the United States, that bereavement is more often to be found leading to delinquency than family break-up or divorce. In the United Kingdom, some psychiatric workers consider that the worst cases of maladjustments in children tend to have a history of bereavement. This says something about how a parent's death may affect the mind, but it also suggests that other situations, where a mother, a mother substitute, or a father can rebuild a close relationship after a false start, are by no means without hope.

The two great obstacles to such a rebuilding programme are pressures of time and over-civilization. A disturbed child needs time given to him, preferably by his parents, in which he can gradually get the message that his parents regard him as important and competent as a companion. This doesn't mean long question-and-answer sessions, which may be intimidating. For the most part, it means being close to him and sharing in what he wants to do; offering help with a broken toy, irrespective of the number of times he breaks it; offering ideas or spending time together—football, jigsaws, painting, or whatever; taking the time. also, to consider what the child is really concerned about, and interpreting what his often babyish talk or behaviour is getting at (for example, he may want cuddling but be too embarrassed to ask because it is not expected of him). His brothers and sisters need time too: they should be encouraged to join in, and complimented when they make the disturbed child happier.

We are over-civilized in that we cultivate passive forms of entertainment to occupy leisure time. These include television, reading, most spectator sports, and being driven in a car. When father and son watch football and discuss the game afterwards, that is certainly a kind of contact, and it is worth while. But each is discovering more about Manchester United than how each other thinks, shares and acts. Sitting on the floor with a baby requires a greater effort of will than watching him while ringing up a friend on the telephone. Anyone with a disturbed child will get closer to him by participating in activities with him, rather than sharing passive entertainment.

A distinction has to be drawn between paying attention to a child, and pandering to his whims and allowing anti-social behaviour. To do the latter may mean perpetuating a system of unproductive compensations which end up by infuriating everybody. How to draw the distinction must be a matter for the individual parent's judgment, but every child benefits from having some part of the day in which he can act in an unfettered, possibly anti-social, way. The great popularity at fairgrounds of stalls where you pay for the privilege of smashing plates attests to this.

Nor is paying attention the same as spoiling. John Bowlby—whose work on the subject of maternal care is probably more extensive and authoritative than anyone else's—suggests that there is a parallel between the questions of how much attention a child should get and how much food. On food, children are great self-regulators (in the amount, if not the type of food they demand) unless they have a faulty metabolism, or have been ill. Similarly, if they demand more attention, they probably need it. To carry Bowlby's parallel further: just as a period of under-nourishment requires initiative from the mother to correct the situation gradually, so a serious break in attention needs to be repaired, by the mother's initiative, over a period of time.

One major goal in bringing the relationship back towards normal is to get the child to talk about, or enact, the feelings he had, and was frightened by, during a bad separation experience. This cannot be forced. Direct questioning will achieve nothing. What is needed is a lot of patience, until the subject can come up more or less naturally. By this time the child will recognize and perhaps temper his condemnation of the parents who 'let him down' at separation.

All this helps. But nobody can assess the problems in a situation with the same objectivity as that of a social worker, if they are inside that situation. When a child is disturbed after separation and the recovery seems slow or incomplete, it is often sensible to ask for some aid from outside. Many parents are very loth to approach a Child Guidance Clinic until a child is very disturbed. Obviously, demanding to see a psychiatrist at the slightest suspicion of a problem is absurd, but there is absolutely no stigma attached to attending the local Child Guidance Clinic. Going sooner, rather than later, may make a lot of difference. Where disturbance is real, and serious, there is no substitute for qualified professional advice.

Bereavement has been mentioned above as a contributory factor in many cases of maladjustment. Often there is a problem of interpretation involved: that is to say, the reading that the child puts into the disappearance of his parent. An unfortunate by-product of the natural inclination of relations to protect the child from the detail of the parent's death is that he does not know what to make of it. Some children grow up with a conviction that they were in some way partly responsible; or that it was disappearance rather than death, and so they imagine strange scenes of return, some of which they hope for, ardently.

It is questionable whether adults, when they arrange for a young child not to go to his parent's funeral, are thinking of the effect on the child, or the effect on themselves and other adults, of having to contemplate the reality of orphanhood. There is a similar question about their motives for changing the subject when the child asks about the death, the funeral, and so forth. Just as refusal to discuss matters of sex encourages speculation about the subject that may take peculiar and unfortunate turns, refusal to discuss the permanent disappearance of a much-loved parent, must have similar if not greater effects. Case history records show that disturbed adults who lost a parent as a child, and felt that loss keenly, often bear a long-standing grudge about not being allowed to attend the funeral.

A bereaved child should have his curiosity satisfied, in a sensitive way. He may not be emotionally prepared for a complete funeral service, but it helps if he is involved to some extent, and he certainly deserves to have a special arrangement, however inconvenient or embarrassing to the adults, made for this.

If a parent is ill, particularly the mother, the bereavement problem may be repeated on a smaller scale. Again, sufficient information should be given the child to make it reasonably clear that he himself is not to blame. Again, access ought not to be denied, but if the circumstances of the illness or injury are harrowing, or if there is de-personalization as a result of drugs, or a serious mental handicap, this needs very careful thought. The principle of avoiding mystery by answering questions and giving progress reports is sound, but volunteering alarming data, e.g. that the mother is dying of cancer, had best be avoided. Misleading reports, on the other hand, can be a cruel form of deception, and will probably reduce the credibility of anyone who needs to act as a mother-substitute.

During a mother's enforced absence a young child needs attention as well as basic care. This should be from an individual who is reasonably familiar. If it can be made clear to the child that the arrangements for being looked after while his mother is in hospital have her approval, he will have a feeling of continuity. If she has had an accident, of course, this is very difficult. But in addition to working out which hospital might be best for the child, should he need one, it makes sense to have an idea about who could look after him, in which house, before the parents have an accident. It goes without saying that if there were a better feeling of community, as advocated above, there would be a better chance of children being looked after by neighbours in friendly and familiar surroundings.

Few things are as capable of unfortunate misinterpretation as a mother leaving a young child to go into hospital and returning with a baby. Not only is there abandonment—for something done wrong?—but a rival is brought back to supplant his position permanently.

It is no bad thing that in the United Kingdom the majority of confinements, after the first, take place at home. This practice, which is frowned on as being unnecessarily risky by some other countries, makes it more obvious that the event is to be a family one. As much as possible should be done to make a child feel that the newcomer is the family's baby, not just mummy's. Dr Spock's advice on buying a 'birthday present' for the other child, or children, goes some way towards sugaring the pill that attention is now going to be further divided.

*   *   *

These suggestions are much easier to make, and to accept, against the background of a society that really likes children. But do the British like children? The evidence makes one believe that although they are better than most at keeping children alive, they are disinclined to enjoy their company. The nation that developed the boarding-school and the nannie as great institutions, and sends its children to school earlier than most others, is suspect in this respect.

The same point can be made when considering the conditions described in the earlier chapters. Why else has it taken so long to implement the Platt Report recommendations? Or to plan the phasing out of large, isolated hospitals? Or to squeeze more money to improve the ratio of nursing and teaching staff to sick children in long-stay hospitals? Why are handicapped or abnormal children pitied, then forgotten, rather than given the help to become integrated in society?

Sitting at a table in a square in Valletta, I was recently struck by the noise and happiness at a table nearby. Three children were drinking cola, and having a lot of fun. Adults close to them had to stop talking, every now and then, to let the laughter die down. But there were no impatient glares.

Not having a word of Maltese, it took me a few minutes to realize that one of the three was mentally handicapped. He may well have been autistic. One of the two girls was teasing him, and the other was taking his side. They were entirely good-natured, however. The boy seemed to have only a few words, but he used them to effect, and supplemented this with the occasional cuff, delivered over the table. Whether they were related or not was difficult to say, but it was obvious that they were used to each other's company, and enjoyed life together, at least on Sunday morning, after church. Together, they formed an island of liveliness, which the local regulars indulged, with an occasional shout of encouragement.

The only other Anglo-Saxons on the terrace looked decidedly uncomfortable.

References and Bibliography

CHAPTER 1. PREMATURE SEPARATION

J. Bowlby, *Child Care and the Growth of Love*. Harmondsworth: Penguin Books, 2nd edition, 1965.

Attachment and Loss: vol. i, *Attachment*. Hogarth Press, 1969; Penguin Books, 1971. Vol. ii, *Separation: Anxiety and Anger*. Hogarth Press, 1973.

A. M. Schrier, H. F. Harlow and F. Stollnitz (eds.), *Behaviour of Non-Human Primates*. New York and London, Academic Press, 1965.

CHAPTERS 2 & 3. SHORT-TERM STAY IN HOSPITAL

J. Robertson, *Hospitals and Children: A Parent's Eye View*. Gollancz, 1963.

Young Children in Hospital—with Postscript 1970. Tavistock Publications, 1970.

D. J. Brain and I. Maclay, 'Controlled Study of Mothers and Children in Hospital' (the Rubery Hill Report). *British Medical Journal*. 3 February 1968.

Report on the Welfare of Children in Hospital (the Platt Report). HMSO, 1958.

Hospital Facilities for Children. DHSS Memorandum, HMSO, April 1971.

FOR INTRODUCING CHILDREN TO HOSPITAL PRACTICE:

Ages 2–7:

M. and H. A. Rey, *Zozo Goes to Hospital*. Chatto and Windus, 1967.

Children's Hospital Painting Book. National Association for the Welfare of Children in Hospital, 1972.

Age 8 plus:

A. Weber, *Lisa Goes to Hospital*. Blackie, 1970.

CHAPTER 4. LONG-TERM STAY IN HOSPITAL

M. Oswin: *The Empty Hours, A Study of the Weekend Life of Handicapped Children in Institutions*. Allen Lane, The Penguin Press, 1971.

H. Geiger, *The Family in Soviet Russia*. Oxford University Press, 1966.

J. Parfit: *Spotlight on Services for the Young Handicapped Child*. National Children's Bureau, 1972.

CHAPTERS 5 & 6. FAMILY BREAK-UP

J. Eekelaar, *Family Security and Family Breakdown*. Harmondsworth: Penguin Books, 1971.

M. Wynn, *Fatherless Families*. Michael Joseph, 1964.

J. T. Landis, 'The Trauma of Children Whose Parents Divorce'. *Marriage and Family Living*, vol. 22, 1966.

S. and E. Gluech, *Unravelling Juvenile Delinquency*. Oxford University Press, 1950.

R. Davie, N. Butler and H. Goldstein, *From Birth to Seven*. 2nd Report of the National Child Development Study (especially Chapter 4). National Children's Bureau, 1972.

FOR ADVICE AND HELP:

Gingerbread, 9 Poland Street, London W1V 3DG (an association for one-parent families).

CHAPTER 7. FOSTERING AND ADOPTION

R. Dinnays and M. L. Kelmer Pringle, *Foster Home Care: Facts and Fallacies*. National Children's Bureau, Longman, 1967.

M. A. Yelloly, 'Factors Relating to an Adoption Decision by the Mothers of Illegitimate Infants'. *Sociological Review*, vol. 13, 1965.

CHAPTER 8. BOARDING-SCHOOLS

Public Schools Commission: 1st Report, HMSO, 1968 (Newsom Commission).

R. Wilkinson, *The Prefects*. Oxford University Press, 1963.

Royston Lambert, *The Hot-House Society*. Weidenfeld & Nicolson, 1968.

CHAPTER 9. MENTAL HANDICAPS

SOCIETIES DEDICATED TO SPECIFIC PROBLEMS:

Association for All Speech Impaired Children (AFASIC), 9 Desenfans Road, Dulwich Village, London SE21.

Association for Spina Bifida and Hydrocephalus, 112 City Road, London EC1.

British Epilepsy Association,
3 Alfred Place, London WC1.
Colombo House for 'Exceptional' Children (for mentally retarded children),
1 Ferry Road, Teddington, Middx.
MacIntyre School and Village for the Severely Mentally Handicapped,
Westoning Manor, Westoning, Nr Flitwick, Beds.
National Association for Deaf/Blind and Rubella Children,
61 Senneleys Park Road, Northfield, Birmingham B31 1AE.
National Deaf Children's Society,
31 Gloucester Place, London W1.
National Society for Autistic Children,
1a Golders Green Road, London NW11.
The Spastics Society,
12 Park Crescent, London WIN 4EQ.

CHAPTER 10. WHAT CAN A PARENT DO ABOUT SEPARATION?
B. Tudor-Hart, *Learning to Live*. Sphere Books, 1968.

Index

Abortion, 92
Adoption, 79 et seq.
Advice:
  on assessing boarding-schools, 57 et seq.
  on family break-up, 70 et seq.
  on long-stay at hospitals, 57 et seq.
  on looking at residential schools, homes, etc., for mentally handicapped children, 130, 131
  on short-stay at hospitals, 38 et seq.
  when child enters boarding-school, 111 et seq.
Age, effects on reacting to separation, 22, 31, 64, 101, 105
Aggressive behaviour, 52, 66
Alienation (after separation), 12, 22
Anxiety (communicated by parents) 23, 26, 136
Attendance allowance, 129
Attention, demand for, 52, 55, 68, 83
Autism, autistic child, 113, 117

Bath, on admission, 18, 27, 28
Betty (case history), 48 et seq.

Bill (case history), 52
Boarding-school, 75, 96 et seq., 128, 129
Bob (case history), 98 et seq.
Bowlby, John, 138
Brain, D. J., and Maclay, Inga, 32
Brain damage, 119

Cathy (case history), 27
Child Guidance Centre, Clinic, 93, 125, 137, 139
Children's home, 80
Children's Officer, 72, 123
Children's ward, 26, 28, 45, 57, 58
Citizens' Advice Bureaux, 57, 72
Class consciousness, 96
Co-education, 109
Compulsions (after separation), 9
Concentration, lack of, 53, 55

Death of parent, 137, 139, 140
Delinquency, 69, 137
Derek (case history), 44 et seq.
Disturbed children, 127, 138
Divorce, 59 et seq.
Douglas and his mother (case history), 88 et seq.

Education Act, 1971, 56
Education for children in hospital, 43, 46
ESN (Educationally Subnormal), 127

Family atmosphere (in boarding-school), 109
Family Benefits, 72
Family group, 48, 106
Family Income Supplement, 72
Fantasy (about parents), 54, 68, 84
Father:
    bringing up child alone, 63
    role of, 87
Fatherless children, 89, 98
Foster parents, 65 et seq., 82
Fostering, 65, 79 et seq., 92
Freud, S., 15

George (case history), 107
Guilt feelings after separation, 14, 62

Harlow, 15
Health Visitor, 93
Hospital, short term stay in, 8 et seq., 16 et seq.
Housemaster, 98, 105

Ian (case history), 8 et seq.
Individuality, 97, 106, 131
Interpretation, of separation, 13, 23, 62

Jealousy, 7, 22
John (case history), 53, 54

Karen (case history), 10
Keller, Helen, 43
Ken (case history), 124 et seq.

Landis, J. T., 60
Local Education Authority, 113
'Long-stay Personality', 46, 52, 55, 57

Maintenance payments, 72
Maralyn (case history), 126 et seq.
Matron (hospital), 46, 49
Matron (school), 61, 101 et seq.
Meg (case history), 102
Mental sub-normality hospital, 123
Mentally handicapped child, 25
    See especially 115 et seq.
Millie (case history), 92
Mini-separation, 6 et seq., 134
Mongol, 118, 124
Mother:
    importance of presence in hospital, 32
    mother-substitute, 14, 49, 62, 92, 109
    See especially 3 et seq., et passim
Mrs T. and Mrs R. (case history), 34 et seq.

National Association for the Welfare of Children in Hospital (NAWCH), 33, 38

National Council for the Un-married Mother and her Child (NCUMC), 91
National Marriage Guidance Council (NMGC), 70
National Society for Autistic Children (NSAC), 26, 132
National Society for Mentally Handicapped Children (NSMHC), 25, 118, 125
Naughty behaviour, 68
Need achievement, 85
Newsom Commission, 110, 113
Nicholas (case history), 20 et seq.
Nicola (case history), 76
Nursery school, 71

Operation, 18, 20, 30, 40
Orwell, George, 97
Oswin, Maureen, 56
Over-nighting (by mother in hospital), 21, 29, 33, 35
Over-protection, 32

Parent's illness, 92, 140
Personality change. See Long-stay Personality,
Philip (case history), 65 et seq.
Platt Report, 33, 34, 141
Play group, 48
Precociousness, 68, 86
Premature separation, 3 et seq.
'Pre-med', 21, 29
Preparations (before entry into hospital), 38, 39

Psychiatric hospital, 123
Psychiatrist, 9, 77, 85, 117, 128
Psychologist, 3, 7, 127
Punishment, separation inter-preted as, 13, 62

Refusing food, 120
Regression after separation, 8, 41, 47, 123
Rejection, separation inter-preted as, 13, 62, 94, 104
Repression of feelings, 98
Resentment, of mother towards child, 75
Residential school, centre, 43, 54, 76. See also Children's home
Return home from hospital, behaviour on, 8, 19–21, 37, 41, 47
Robertson, James, 29
Robin (case history), 17 et seq.
Role of nurses, parents, 23, 28, 29, 40
Rubery Hill Report, 32, 33
Rules, hospital, 36, 40

Sally (case history), 35 et seq.
Schizophrenia, 116
Self-reliance, 5, 100
Separation, husband and wife, 53, 59 et seq., 101. See also Premature separation
Settling down, in hospital, 35, 47
Shirley (case history), 53
Shyness, 53, 66

Siblings of handicapped child, 128, 129
Social behaviour, 55, 104, 126
Social worker, 48, 49, 63, 70, 91
Spastics Society, 26
'Specialed' nurse, 21, 28, 48
Speech difficulty, 120
Spock, Dr B., 141
Status, concern about, 95
Stealing, 66
Stepfather, 89

Tantrum after separation, 19, 41, 47
Tavistock Institute, 15
Teacher (in hospital), 49 et seq., 66, 67

Thalidomide, 42
Tim (case history), 119
Time, child's sense of, 30
Training centre, 124

Under-developed countries, 23
Unreality of life in hospital, 43, 47

Visiting children in hospital, 16, 30, 33, 37, 39
Visits to hospital, 122

Ward Sister, 19, 20, 28, 34, 35, 37
Will (case history), 67 et seq.